GRAMMAR TO GO

THE PORTABLE A–ZED GUIDE TO CANADIAN USAGE
3RD EDITION

Rob Colter

ANANSI

First published in 1978 by House of Anansi Press Ltd.
Revised edition published in 1981 by House of Anansi Press Ltd.

Third edition published in 2005 by House of Anansi Press Inc.
110 Spadina Avenue, Suite 801, Toronto, ON, M5V 2K4
Tel. 416-363-4343 Fax 416-363-1017 www.anansi.ca

Distributed in Canada by
HarperCollins Canada Ltd.
1995 Markham Road
Scarborough, ON, M1B 5M8
Toll free tel. 1-800-387-0117

Distributed in the United States by
Publishers Group West
1700 Fourth Street
Berkeley, CA 94710
Toll free tel. 1-800-788-3123

09 08 07 06 05   1 2 3 4 5

LIBRARY AND ARCHIVES CANADA CATALOGUING IN PUBLICATION DATA

Colter, Rob, 1945–
Grammar to go : the portable A-Zed guide to Canadian usage/
Rob Colter. — 3rd ed.

ISBN 0-88784-723-4

1. English language — Grammar. I. Title.

PE1112.C58 2004   428.2   C2004-905558-5

Cover design: Bill Douglas at The Bang
Cover photograph: Getty Images/Brand X Pictures
Text design and typesetting: Tannice Goddard

Canada Council
for the Arts
Conseil des Arts
du Canada

ONTARIO ARTS COUNCIL
CONSEIL DES ARTS DE L'ONTARIO

*We acknowledge for their financial support of our publishing
program the Canada Council for the Arts, the Ontario Arts Council,
and the Government of Canada through the Book Publishing
Industry Development Program (BPIDP).*

Printed and bound in Canada

CONTENTS

PREFACE TO THE THIRD EDITION

Welcome to the third edition of *Grammar to Go: The Portable A–Zed Guide to Canadian Usage*, which contains 25 new entries and updated explanations and examples. What's Canadian about it? Well, the pronunciation of "Z," for one thing, but since Canadian English usage is not identical with either American or British usage, especially in spelling, vocabulary, and punctuation, these differences are pointed out in the explanations. The new entries address persistent questions that have arisen since the last edition. For example, guidelines are provided for composing e-mail, presenting lists, and eliminating "high carb" phrases. Another new entry offers pointers for the use of inclusive language, and the numerous uses of the slash are now included in the *Punctuation* section.

Of course perennial puzzlers, like "it's" and "its" and "who" and "whom," are still included, because they continue to cause writers trouble. Similarly, there's still lots of confusion about how to form the possessive of nouns (see *Possessive Case*) — and who can remember when to write numbers as figures and not words? In total, answers to these and 225 more questions are provided in this new edition.

A completely new feature is the inclusion of brief quizzes, anecdotes, and quotations related to language, which are interspersed throughout the book. These are meant to both enlighten and entertain, and I hope you enjoy them as much as I (do).

The goal of *Grammar to Go*, however, remains the same as it was with the two previous editions: to provide easy-to-understand answers to common questions of grammar and usage. No one can be expected to remember every detail of correct usage. For academic success and career advancement, however, it is important to use the language correctly, which is why conscientious writers habitually refer to dictionaries and guidebooks like this one.

Those of you already familiar with the book's design will notice that it has been reorganized to make it even easier to use. The four original headings have been retained, but *Spelling* and *Common Confusions* are now combined so that the book contains three sections instead of four. Entries under each of these sections now appear alphabetically within the section. This more consolidated approach means, for example, that all entries related to *Punctuation* are now together in one location.

In the Contents, when entries for *Grammar and Style* are identified by their grammatical term they are often accompanied by a familiar example. Page references have been retained.

Grammar to Go is not a comprehensive treatment of grammar, style, punctuation or spelling, nor is it the last word on any of these subjects, but that is not what most writers are looking for. I hope you will enjoy this book and find it useful, and may it stimulate you to learn even more about our language.

— *Rob Colter*
Toronto
September 2005

My thanks to everyone at Anansi,
both past and present,
for their support.

GRAMMAR AND STYLE

Grammar: that dreaded word. Who hasn't shuddered at the thought of having to learn it? Ask for a definition of boring, and this would be near the top of the list. Why? Because it's usually taught like math is taught — all rules and no fun. But writing (like golf or carpentry) is a skill, and you need some knowledge and a lot of practice to become good at it. If you think of it this way, then avoiding a sentence fragment will become as relevant as avoiding 3-putts in your golf game.

If grammar embodies the fundamentals of the game, then *style* describes the way you play it. Are your sentences smooth or awkward? Do you care whether "impact" is a poor choice as a verb, or that "hopefully" does not mean, "I hope"? Do you express yourself clearly and effectively, making every word and sentence count?

Leaders on Grammar
"Even Kings must obey the laws of grammar."
— MOLIÈRE (1622–1673)

"I will not go down to posterity talking bad grammar."

— BENJAMIN DISRAELI (1804–1881)

"I stand by all the misstatements that I've made."
— GOVERNOR GEORGE W. BUSH (1946–)

ADMIT
When used to mean "confess," it is never followed by "to."

> He admitted his mistake.
> He admits having done it.
> He admits it.

ADVERBS (GO SLOW)
Some people get awfully bugged because GO SLOW signs do not read "Go Slowly," but as a combined warning to "go slow and slow down," they convey the intended message, even to strict grammarians.

DRIVE CAREFUL (be careful when you drive) is less defensible, in speech "do it right" is barely okay, and phrases like "awful bugged," "real hungry," "do it gentle," "wash it good," and "take it slow" are really lousy.

Just remember that words that describe verbs (and adjectives and other adverbs) almost always end in "ly." Well, "very," and "fast" are common exceptions. (And so is "well.")

AMONG/BETWEEN

"*Between* two, *among* three or more" is a useful rule worth remembering. However, when the interaction between individual members of a group is stressed, "between," not "among," is the sensible word. Thus, "an agreement between (many) nations," since each agrees with the other, is more forceful than the rather vague "among nations."

AMOUNT/NUMBER

Certain things can be counted and they have plural forms; certain things cannot be counted and they don't have plural forms.

For countables, use *number*; for uncountables, use *amount*.

The number of cars . . .
The amount of time, beer, wine, etc.

When these are misused — "the amount of people" — it makes you wonder why this is any easier than saying it the right way.

Note:

> The number of carpenters *is* increasing.

> But:

> A number of carpenters *are* eating lunch outside.

In the first example, *number* refers to a single unit; in the second, *number* refers to some members of that unit. (For other collectives see *Collective Nouns*. For diminished quantity, see *Less/Fewer*.)

APOSTROPHE

The apostrophe performs three functions:

1. It indicates an omitted letter (or letters) when two words are contracted:

   'Twas the night before Christmas. . . .

   The most common of these contractions are the personal pronouns with the verb "to be":

I am	I'm
you are	you're
she is	she's
he is	he's
it is	it's

we are	we're
you are	you're
they are	they're

A sampling of others:

is not	isn't
are not	aren't
do not	don't
does not	doesn't
did not	didn't
I would	I'd
would not	wouldn't
cannot	can't
could not	couldn't
should not	shouldn't

(See *Could of/Would of.*)

Because they are used in conversation, contractions impart an informal tone and therefore are avoided in formal writing, which includes all external, and most internal, business communication.

2. It indicates the possessive form in both the singular and plural (see *Possessive Case*).

3. It indicates the plural form of letters, but not of figures (see *Plurals*, #4).

Dot your i's and cross your t's.
Remember the 1960s?

> "If all the grammarians in the world were
> placed end to end, it would be a good thing."
>
> — UNKNOWN

AS FAR AS . . . CONCERNED

As far as the landing on the moon, I think it
was a waste of time.
As far as the economy, I think it stinks.

If you're willing to accept that, then you should be
willing to accept "As far as George, he couldn't care
less." Are you?

The right way is, "As far as George is concerned,
he couldn't care less." And the first sentence should
read, "As far as the landing on the moon is concerned, I think it was a waste of time."

More and more people are not bothering to
end with "concerned" when they begin with "as far
as." Maybe they think they are saying "as for."
Whatever the reason, we should be concerned.

> ***Couple Gets Nine Months For Caging
> Adopted Sons***
> announces the newspaper headline, then begins
> the story with, "*An Ontario couple have been
> sentenced. . . .*"
> Obviously the headline writer and the reporter
> don't agree on whether "couple" is a singular or
> plural noun. What's the guideline?
> (See *Collective Nouns* p. 11)

BEG THE QUESTION

Begging the question does not mean that you
deliberately avoid answering a question, but that the
evidence you are using as proof for your conclusion
is simply a restatement of your conclusion.

The most common variety of this is the circular
argument. (Today often called a Catch-22, particularly if it describes one of officialdom's circuitous
procedures.)

> Mothers love their babies because they have a
> maternal instinct.

And, as an infamous politician once said:

> We will stop bombing their cities when they
> stop shooting down our bombers.

BEING

Avoid using *being* as a replacement for "since" or "because," and avoid the phrases "being as" and "being that." There are much better (and simpler) ways of saying what you mean.

> Being a student, I must live on limited funds.
> Being late, we had to hurry.
> He disagrees, his reason being that these are
>   personal issues.

All of these sentences can be much more strongly expressed.

> Since I'm a student, I must live on limited
>   funds.
> We had to hurry because we were late.
> He disagrees, because these are personal issues.

CAPITALIZATION

There are plenty of rules concerning capitalization, but little consistency among them. Generally, you can defend the use of capitals on the grounds that the reference is to a particular and unique person or thing. Thus, "The St. Lawrence River," but "the St. Lawrence and Saguenay rivers."

Do not capitalize:
1. The seasons. Fall (not autumn) is optional:

    spring, summer, autumn, winter

2. Government, when it is not identified by an adjective:

    the British Government
    Leadership in the government steadily
        worsened.

Capitalize:
1. Personal names; titles or rank; organizations, corporations, government departments:

    Elmer Fudd; Admiral Jones, the Victorian
    Order of Nurses; International Business
    Machines; the Ministry of National
    Defence; Prime Minister Martin (but,
    "Martin is prime minister"); President
    Clinton (but, "Clinton was president")

2. Races; languages; geographical names and regions:

    the Australians; the English language;
    Florida, the West, the deep South

3.   Particular streets, buildings, parks, etc.:

King Street, the CN Tower, Stanley Park

4.   Planets and stars; gods and religious writings:

Pluto, the Milky Way; Buddha, the Bible

5.   Particular schools and school courses:

He went to university.
He went to Queen's University.
He took Animal Noises 204.

6.   Brand names and publications:

Shake 'n Bake; *Scientific American*

7.   Days, months, holidays:

Monday, March, Christmas

8.   Historic events and periods:

the Dark Ages, the Renaissance, World
War II.

COLLECTIVE NOUNS (COUPLE IS/ARE)

Do you say "The couple *is* having problems" or "The couple *are* having problems"? "The Merrydale City Council *have* [or *has*?] decided to ban the sale of certain magazines"?

Whether you think of the noun as singular or plural depends on whether you see it as a collection of individuals or as individual members of a group.

If you know the couple next door and think of them as "they," most likely you would say, "the couple are . . .," whereas if their concerns were more remote from you, you would probably think of them in a less personal way, as a couple: "that couple is . . ."

Similarly, if you are acquainted with members of the Merrydale City Council, you would see the council as "they" rather than "it."

In general, the use of the singular makes the noun impersonal, while the plural makes it personal by recognizing the members of the collective.

The British tend to use the plural — "the British Government are making inquiries" — while Canadians and Americans tend to use the singular — "the crowd was unruly."

Note that because corporations are generally seen as impersonal entities — "IBM has offices around the world" — pains are taken to make their image more personal.

We at XYZ Co. know your needs.

Expressions such as "clump of maples," "flock of geese," "herd of elephants" usually take a singular verb, as the members of such collectives are not generally thought of as individuals.

The flock of geese has disappeared.

But:

The geese have disappeared.

> "From now on, ending a sentence with a preposition is something up with which I will not put."
>
> — WINSTON CHURCHILL (1874–1965)

CONDITIONAL MOOD (IF I WOULD HAVE KNOWN)

Today we often hear, "If I would have known, I would have done it differently."

The little word "if," which signals a condition, is the clue to the form of the verb in such sentences. The condition expressed can be real ("if this, then that") or unreal ("if this were true, then that would be true"). As you can see, the first has a possibility of being fulfilled, but the second is only a speculation.

1. If there is a chance the action will take place, put the first verb after "if" in the *present* tense:

    If I know the answers, I'll pass the test. (I might know them, and I might not.)

2. If there is no chance the action will take place, use the *past* tense of the verb:

    If I knew the answers (but I don't), I would pass the test.

    The past tense is used to indicate the unreality of the statement. Note also that "would" does not appear in the "if" clause.

3. If there *was* no chance the action would take place, use the *double past tense* of the verb:

    If I had known the answers (but I didn't), I would have passed the test.

Applying this progression to the introductory example results in, "If I had known, I would have done it differently."

(Examples #2 and #3 are contrary to fact. See *Subjunctive Mood* for more examples.)

DANGLING MODIFIERS

Make sure that *modifiers* clearly relate to the person or thing you have in mind.

> Having eaten our dinner, the dog wanted to go for a walk.

The above sentence means that the dog, having eaten our dinner, wanted to go for a walk. What you probably meant to say was, "After we had eaten, the dog wanted to go for a walk."

> When a boy, Dad played hockey with me.

Dad, when a boy, played hockey with you? You meant, "When I was a boy, Dad . . ."

> Sauntering down the street, a car suddenly
>   burst into flames.
> (While I was sauntering down the street, a
>   car . . .)

> Refusing to stand at attention during the
>   national anthem, the teacher sent him to
>   the principal's office.
> (The teacher sent him to the principal's office
>   for refusing to stand at attention.)

DEAD RULES

1. Never end a sentence with a preposition.

Nonsense! say the authors of the following statements:

> A preposition is not a word to end a sentence with.

> That's a rule up with which I will not put!

> What did you bring me that book to be read to out of for?

And they're right. The "rule" sprang from an insistence on adhering strictly to the rules of Latin, but today that one's as dead as dead can be (it killed the ancient Romans, and now it's killing me).

2. Never begin a sentence with "and" or "but."

This "rule" was instituted to scare off would-be writers of sentence fragments such as the following:

> We went downtown. And bought skis and ski boots.

However, to emphasize concluding or contrary statements, there is nothing wrong with beginning a sentence with "and" or "but," as long as you don't overdo it:

> He concluded his talk by saying that, if re-elected, he would definitely try to do a better job.

> But this promise came too late.

3. Never split infinitives.

Another Latin leftover, referring to the situation in which an infinitive form — "to work" — is separated by one or more words — "to lazily and reluctantly work." But there is nothing wrong with splitting infinitives, as long as you use common sense and your ear.

And there are times when the precise use of the word necessitates splitting the infinitive.

> He tried to gently pry it loose.

Sometimes, however, the word or phrase is simply poorly placed within the sentence. "He tried to not only rob a bank," for instance, can be much better said as, "He not only tried to rob. . . ."

DOCUMENTING SOURCES

If you have relied on sources other than yourself for your information, you must credit these sources at each point in your text where you quote or paraphrase from them. You are also obliged to provide a list of all your sources at the end of your document. If you don't include this information, then you are claiming someone's material as your own, which is theft of intellectual property. Lack of documentation will also prevent your readers from accessing your sources and learning about your subject to the fullest extent possible.

There are two critical parts to any docmentation process: (1) in-text acknowledgements ("citations") at the exact point where the borrowed material is used, whether paraphrased or quoted; and (2) the details of each source used, which are provided in a list ("Works Cited," or "References") at the end of the document.

Formal documentation is required for all scholarly papers, whether in the sciences or the humanities, as well as in all professional reports such as technical reports.

Several different documentation styles are in current use, each with its own distinctive format. These styles have evolved to support different academic or scientific disciplines. The details of these are beyond the scope of this book, but most academic institutions and professional bodies use either the *APA (Publication Manual of the American Psychological Society)* or *MLA (Modern Language Association Handbook for Writers of Research Papers)* documentation systems, or variations of them. The key characteristic of both is that the source is identified immediately in the text.

APA PARENTHETICAL CITATION STYLE

The surname of the author and the date of publication, separated by a comma, are enclosed in parentheses. If the material is quoted, the page reference follows. Sources are then listed in alphabetical order under *References* in the back matter of the document.

One author:
> . . . tensile strength determines shear strength (Boxma, 1993).

One author, quoted:
> " . . . shear strength of steel beams are between 2 and 5% to of the tensile strength, respectively" (Boxma, 1993, p. 63).

Corporation cited:
> "It is estimated that the number of two-car families will double in the next ten years" (ABC Corporation 1992 Annual Report).

Web page cited:

> Over time, NASA officials began to accept
> what was termed a "normalization of deviance"
> (http://caib.nasa.gov/news/report/volume1/
> html).

APA "REFERENCES" STYLE

List sources in alphabetical order, by surname:

> Carswell, K. (2003). *When Bridges Become
> Elastic.* Toronto: Engineering Institute
> Publications.

For web pages, list the surname of the author (if
known); the publication and its date (if known); the
title of the article cited; the latest date you visited it;
and the URL:

> Report of Columbia Accident Investigation
> Board, Vol.1, Chapt. 8 (2003). *The Normaliza-
> tion of Deviance.* Retrieved May 20, 2004, from
> http://www.nasa.gov/columbia/home/CAIB

MLA PARENTHETICAL CITATION STYLE

The surname of the author and the page number,
with no comma.

One author:
> . . . tensile strength determines shear strength
> (Boxma 63).

The same style applies for directly quoted material.

Corporation cited:
> "It is estimated that the number of two-car
> families will double in the next ten years"
> (ABC Corporation 88).

Web page cited:
> Over time, NASA officials began to accept
> what was termed a "normalization of
> deviance" ("Columbia" 196).

MLA "WORKS CITED" STYLE

> Carswell, K. When Bridges Become Elastic.
> Toronto: Engineering Institute Publications,
> 2003.

(Note that the only difference from APA style is the placement of the year.)

For web pages, list the surname of the author (if known); the publication and its date (if known); the title of the article; the latest date you visited it; and the URL. Note how this differs in presentation from

MLA style:

> Report of Columbia Accident Investigation
> Board, Vol.1, Chapt. 8 (2003). The
> Normalization of Deviance. 20 May 2004
> <http://www.nasa.gov/columbia/home/CAIB>.

You will find APA, MLA, and other documentation styles fully explained at the web site of any university or professional association. For formal academic papers, it would be in your best interest to seek further sources beyond this brief overview.

DOUBLE NEGATIVES

"Don't use no double negatives" not only sounds brainless, but means "use double negatives." Two negatives result in a positive or affirmative statement, thus reversing the writer's original meaning. Usually, as in the example given above, the mistake is obvious — it grates on the ear, it is immediately recognized to be lousy English. Other frequently heard examples:

> I haven't got no money.
> I don't have none.
> Don't never make that mistake again.
> He doesn't know nothing.
> She doesn't see nobody anymore.

But, "not" placed before a negative word can create a subtle shade of meaning:

> Louis Riel was not without education.
> (The double negative conveys the sense that
> his level of education was very rudimentary
> but worth nothing.)

> It's not so unusual that rich kids steal from
> their parents. (But it should be!)

Here's another example:

> Bus service to Eganville was not as infrequent
> as he had expected.

This does not mean that bus service was frequent, of course, but that his negative expectation had been overturned. Such double negatives are perfectly permissible and add shades of meaning not obtainable through the use of the appropriate single positive or negative words.

EITHER . . . OR/NEITHER . . . NOR

Because *either* and *neither* refer to one or the other of two things (never more), the verb that accompanies them is always singular.

Either Shivani or Ballu takes out the garbage every Monday morning.

Neither Harry nor Calvin is responsible for this mess.

The use of *neither . . . nor* sometimes causes trouble and the following should help:

1. *Nor* always follows *neither* to express continued negation.

   He was neither handsome nor intelligent.
   (Or: He was not handsome or intelligent.)

2. *Nor* is also used alone to express continued negation.

   In the classroom he had little patience or enthusiasm, and little understanding of his material; nor did he have any desire to impart his slim knowledge to anyone.

   As it turned out, he didn't get the job, nor were things as bad as he had imagined.

3. Multiple objects of a negative verb can be connected by *or* instead of *nor*:

She can't play the piano or sing.
I don't like potato chips or French fries.

Be on the lookout for a negative verb and avoid mistakes like these:

The fact that I am pampered doesn't help too. (either)

Both (neither) of my parents could not read or write English.

E-MAIL

Everyone who uses e-mail knows that it is overused and misused, yet impossible to live without. In a business context, its danger is that it invites a spontaneous response that can lead to hasty composition and an unsuitable level of informality. (It's not surprising that e-mail gave birth to "emotives" within a few years of its existence while, in 500 years of print, they surfaced, sort of, only in cartoons.)

In the following example, the need for communication training in this organization is readily apparent!

Subject: Communication Training for
Employee's

Heres the feedback. Most of the managers, think
the clerical staff should improve their grammer
and punctuation skills yet some of the sec's
say that there bosses constantly ask them to
correct they're errors and rewrite sentences.
So perhaps it would be a good idea, to offer
a coarse to each of these groups, unless
we combined them, many also think they could
use more training with e-mail and business
presentations. Listening skills in meetings and
with clients was also mentioned. When would
this course be offered, mornings, afternoons,
all day? Several sessions would be required. We
should probably wait until the fall because,
so many are on holidays now. We also need to
decide who to hire to teach the coarse, weather
a company or an individual. That's about it.
Let me know if you need any more information.

The most noticeable flaws in this e-mail are its poor
spelling, punctuation, and sentence structure. The
writer simply took no care to conform to standard
English usage. The content is also very disorganized
and presented as an unbroken series of observations.
These should be grouped by headings — variations
on **who**, **what**, **where**, **why**, **when**, and **how** spring

to mind. If that requires more than one computer screen, or if the layout is complex, then the report should be attached as a file.

Guidelines for e-mail:

- Create an accurate and informative subject line.
- Organize and connect information, as you would in the print medium.
- Use an appropriate amount of *white space.
- If you fill more than one screen, consider attaching the message as a file.
- Use standard grammar and spelling.
- Stick to the subject at hand.
- Avoid columns and similar design features.

*White space refers to the unfilled areas on the page. The e-mail example on the previous page is presented as a solid block of featureless text. No subject headings or other breaks in the text indicate the end of one point and the beginning of another. The absence of white space means that the layout is both uninviting and unhelpful to the reader.

> "The greater part of the world's troubles are due to questions of grammar."
> — MICHEL DE MONTAIGNE (1533–1592)

EUPHEMISMS

All languages employ synonyms to reduce the impact of taboo words or words that have unpleasant connotations. Thus, English has hundreds of *euphemisms* for death, sex, and toilet functions: "passed on," "sleep with," or "the men's room." To explain how the bare breast of a female entertainer came to be revealed to millions of surprised viewers, the phrase "wardrobe malfunction" was coined. War and weapons are also heavily euphemized — "nuke" for nuclear, "incursion" for invasion. During the Vietnam War, "Operation Rolling Thunder" gave a poetic ring to the bombing of Hanoi.

In recent years governments have resorted more and more to employing euphemisms (and "consultants"): "stimulative deficit" and "misspeak" are now in common usage. People used to be unqualified for certain jobs, then they were "under-qualified." Now they are more likely to be described as "overqualified." "Unemployment insurance" has given way to the more positive (but contradictory) "employment insurance."

Sometimes a deliberate change of terms can help to replace a negative association or eliminate bias. For example, over the past 50 years, a succession of terms have been coined to describe physical disability, each being replaced as it acquired a negative connotation: "handicapped," "disabled," "physically challenged," and, most recently, "diversely abled." Each in turn was intended to promote greater acceptance and inclusiveness. (See *Inclusive Language*.)

Euphemisms reflect the sensitive areas of contemporary society, and a comprehensive catalogue of them would reveal a great deal about our socio-political discomforts and fears.

HOPEFULLY

Used widely today to mean "I hope," or "I hope so," it means "in a hopeful manner," so that, "Hopefully I'll see you," is nonsense, though no one will misunderstand what you mean.

Hopefully must be used to describe a verb, so that "he sighed hopefully," "[I remain] hopefully yours," are correct.

There no longer seems to be any point in objecting to its misuse in speech but, until this one is fully accepted, you'd best avoid it in writing.

IF/WHETHER

If is used when a condition exists — *if* this, *then* this.

Whether, on the other hand, simply indicates that a choice exists between one thing and another — "I don't know whether I'll go."

Even though this sentence contains no condition, *if* is frequently used as a synonym for *whether* in such sentences — "I wonder if he'll come."

But in the following examples, *whether* cannot be substituted for *if*, because the sentences state true conditions:

> I'll go if I have the money.
> > (Only if I have the money will I go.)
> We would have stayed if it hadn't rained.

If you're tempted to substitute "whether or not" for *if* in the third example above — "I'll go whether or not I have the money" — notice that you've changed the meaning entirely to say, "I'll go anyway."

I MYSELF THINK

Ah, the indulged self. In an effort to sound humble (it's only my opinion), or pompous (myself, of course), all sorts of people take all sorts of trouble to avoid using "I" all by its lonesome.

Here are some examples:

> I personally think . . .
> Personally, I think . . .
> It's my opinion that . . .
> In my opinion . . .
> In my personal opinion . . .
> Myself, I don't . . .

I myself don't . . .
I don't myself personally care, etc. . . .

For all of these personae, "I think" is simply and clearly what you mean.

Use "in my opinion" only to emphasize that yours is a contrary opinion and, as for the rest, forget 'em.

INCLUSIVE LANGUAGE

Words are labels. They can praise; they can put down. Words can be inclusive, but they can also be exclusive. In this ever-developing global community, more and more we are remarking on the similarities between peoples, rather than noting our differences. The first, and probably most important, step in ensuring that our differences are accorded equal value and respect is to use *inclusive language*.

A brief backward look reveals how conscientiously we have accepted our mission to promote this inclusiveness.

For example, the *Toronto Star Style Book* of June 1954, begins its introduction with a commitment to "kindness and dignity" in reporting, then goes on to say, "All derogatory terms belittling race or religion or otherwise exposing a person to ridicule are forbidden," specifically denouncing several racial terms in popular use at that time.

By 1983, *The Canadian Press Stylebook* lists 11 items under the heading "Sexism," the first point being, "Treat the sexes equally and without stereotyping."

Yet the writers feel obliged to include in the list the statement, "Do not suggest surprise that a woman has talent," as in, "You would never guess from Mary Brown's appearance, but she is a highly regarded brain surgeon."

Another item in the list reads, "It is proper English to let *he* (*him, his*) stand as a word of common or indeterminate gender."

Today, of course, anyone expressing these views would be laughed out of the room.

For several decades this change in attitude has focused on the elimination of sexist language, which has evolved naturally to include the removal of any perceived bias. (See *Euphemisms*.)

For example, the bias implicit in gender-specific occupations, such as "foreman," "stewardess," "fireman," "waiter," "male nurse," was neutralized by the substitution of terms like "supervisor," "flight attendant," "firefighter," "server," and "nurse."

Even though we've had to endure some silliness along the way, and some still label the whole movement as nothing more than an opportunistic attempt at "political correctness," much has been gained in rewiring our psyches to be more tolerant and appreciative of the differences we all carry with us.

So, you ask: Do I still use "he/she," and what pronoun do I use when I start a sentence with "anyone" or "everybody"? And is it "Chairperson" or "Chair" of the committee?

The answer to the first two questions can be found under *Subject-Pronoun Agreement (Everyone Knows His/Their)*.

"Chair" is preferred over "Chairperson" and "Ombuds" over "Ombudsman" for the same reason "his/her" has fallen out of favour; namely, stylistically it just seems too clumsy and artificial to persist with these adaptations. Besides, if you were Chair of a committee, wouldn't you want your correspondence to be headed, "From the desk of the Chair"?

INDIRECT/DIRECT SPEECH

Direct speech is the written or spoken word as it is uttered:

"What's all this hullabaloo?" he asked.

Indirect speech is the written or spoken word as it is reported:

He asked what all the hullabaloo was about.

Naturally, because it's reported, indirect speech always refers to a past action.
Consider:

"I'm never going to trampoline again," he said.

Change to indirect speech:

He said he *was* never going to trampoline again.

Having said that, if you want to emphasize that the speaker still feels this way, you can use the same time as used in the direct statement — in this case, present time:

He says he's never going to trampoline again.

Examples of the change from direct to indirect speech in other verb tenses follow:

Future:

"We'll be there," she insisted.
She insisted they'd be there.
She insists they'll be there.

Past:

"I flipped out at the circus," he said.
He said he had flipped out at the circus.
He says he flipped out at the circus.

Present Perfect:

> "I've never eaten walrus," he confided to her.
> He confided to her that he'd never eaten walrus.
> He says he's never eaten walrus.

Direct speech describes what is happening, *indirect speech* describes what happened, and good story-tellers can describe what happened as though it were happening. Here is a (for us) minor event, told in the three different ways:

> As he was going downstairs, Fernly saw a man in the living room. "What do you want?" asked Fernly, trembling. A smile broke over the burglar's face. "What have you got?"

> As Fernly was coming down the stairs he saw a burglar in the living room. Fernly asked him what he wanted and the guy asked him what he had.

> So Fernly comes waltzing downstairs and he sees this big ape standing in the living room. Fernly asks him what he wants and — get this! — the guy says, "What have you got?"

Notice that the last version is made up of *both* indirect and direct speech. That is fine, as long as you avoid inconsistency:

The president opened the meeting by asking what had gone wrong, *how did we lose the account?* K. replied that it was the client's fault, not ours; Q. agreed, and said maybe *we're better off* without it.

The passage should read:

The president opened the meeting by asking how the account had been lost. K. replied that it had been the client's fault; Q. agreed and thought that perhaps we were better off without it.

When responding in writing to an article, you have the choice of responding in the present tense or the past tense — "The Prime Minister says we will have to tighten our belts" or "The Prime Minister said we will have to tighten our belts" are both correct, but the first choice perhaps signals a greater sense of urgency.

However, if you are evaluating or analyzing an article, the custom is to use the so-called "historical present," which brings the discussion into present time, making it more immediate and fresh: "Freud *says* that we are slaves to our subconscious." If the reference is not the main focus of your discussion, then the tendency is to refer to it in the past tense: "Freud *believed* that . . ."

It's difficult to be consistent about this. Here are some tips: (1) decide whether you are thinking of the event or the passage as "here and now" or as "there and then"; (2) address yourself to the real or mythical reader of your report — "tell" your story to somebody; (3) proofread to ensure that you haven't moved from past to present and back again.

ISSUES

We should definitely take *issue* with the misuse of this word.

It can be used legitimately in reference to the subject matter of debates or points of discussion, as in "the election issues," or "what is at issue here?"

But its use has cascaded downward, becoming a vague shorthand, not only for concrete discussion points, but for sub-points (and beyond) and for multiple concerns:

> The prime minister underlined the following urgent issues: health care, honesty in government, and the continuing war on terrorism.

That's a legitimate use of *issues*. Resist the temptation to continue with "health-care issues," etc. "Health care" *is* the issue; funding and shortage of doctors (for example) are what make this an issue in the first place. When every aspect of every subject is referred to as an *issue*, it is impossible to sort out and deal effectively with any of them.

At a less formal level, the word is used as a catch-all for just about anything that is causing trouble:

I have food issues.

(Meaning allergies, obesity, fear of genetically modified foods?)

I am having conflict issues at work.

(Conflict with whom? About what? Say what you mean!)

The head of Pollution Probe will be speaking about global-warming issues.

(Global warming *is* the issue.)

LATIN ABBREVIATIONS

Ad hoc is invariably used to describe decision-making bodies, such as committees, which are set up to perform a specific function and are then disbanded when their goal has been fulfilled. In this sense, "special committee" is an equivalent, and perhaps more readily understandable than *ad hoc* committee.

(*cf.*) — "compare." *Cf.* is used to point out close similarities or contrasts between words, theories, opinions, or facts:

> Not long after World War II, Germany became the principal industrial centre in Europe (cf. Britain).

e.g., exempli gratia — "for example, for instance."

> Some of the cars of the fifties, *e.g.* the Studebaker, were superbly designed.

et al. — "other people." *Et al.* and *etc.* are not synonyms. Usually *et al.* implies that these people are known to the reader and it is unnecessary to name them.

> The Bloomsbury group — Virginia Woolf, et al. — were a mighty strange lot.

etc., et cetera — "other things." In writing do not use *etc.* as a filler for a lazily presented list:

> We went shopping, etc. this afternoon.

When listing examples of the same class and category, however, *etc.* is a perfect way to cut the list short:

But the larger American cars — Buick,
Lincoln, etc. — are as popular as ever.

i.e., id est — "namely; that is to say." *I.e.,* like *e.g.,* is
much overworked; generally, it is better and clearer
to say "namely."

He called for stronger measures, *i.e.* the return
to the rod, and promised not to spare it.

(q.v.), quod vide — "which see," directs the reader
to a passage elsewhere in the book, or to a relevant
author or text. Equivalents are "(see above)," "(see
below)," and "(see page . . .)."

And, as his mother tells us, he had, at the
time, not only mumps but whooping cough
and measles, to boot *(q.v.* page 22).

re — "in the matter of." Use it only to indicate the
subject of a memorandum. When used within a
sentence, it is simply a lame substitute for "about"
or "regarding."

(sic) — "to follow the copy precisely." It is used
to indicate that errors or apparent errors or
eccentricities of expression are being quoted
faithfully.

He said that "he should have came (*sic*)
earlier."

LATIN PHRASES

ne plus ultra — "nothing beyond," the extreme point.

The Ferrari is often considered to be the
ne plus ultra of automobiles.

quid pro quo — "What for what"; i.e. "something for
something," an equivalent.

The Canadian provinces are becoming
increasingly disenchanted with the
deterioration of a quid pro quo relationship
with Ottawa, the seat of the federal
government.

sine qua non — "without which not (or nothing)."
The essential thing.

The Alaska pipeline appears to be the *sine qua
non* of our future energy reserves.

vice versa — the reverse of the previous meaning

You should be helping her and vice versa.

It was once traditional to insist that all foreign phrases and abbreviations be italicized to "set off" the exotic words. Strict grammarians will also want commas after *i.e.*, *e.g.*, and viz., *etc.*, but this no longer applies.

Other common abbreviations
d. died
b. born
ca. or c. circa, meaning "about," used for dates.
l., ll. line(s)
p., pp. page(s)
ch., chs. chapter(s)
vol., vols. volume(s)
ed., eds. edition(s), editor(s), edited by
no., nos. number(s)
f., ff. and the following page(s)

LESS/FEWER

To express diminished amount, use *less*. To express diminished number, use *fewer*.

Thus:

There are fewer large cars than there were
before.
I now spend less time watching TV.

Never use *less* with a plural noun, as in "less cars, less people." (Supermarkets that have express lines for "less than 8 items" haven't yet heard about this.)

LIKE/AS

"Like" is correctly used to compare objects or persons:

> Wine is like love.
> Frederick eats like a horse.
> Jane smiles like a little girl.

But *like* can never be substituted for *as*, "as if," "as though", or "as . . . as."

> In the ring that year, Romero fought as though he knew he was going to die. (NOT "like he knew . . .")

> Al and Bea talk as if they're going out of business. (NOT "talk like they're . . .")

> We're going to Florida, as we did last year. (NOT "like last year . . .")

Notice in the first examples that when *like* is used correctly, a person or a thing (a noun) immediately follows it:

Doris eats like a bird and sings like my mother.

When "as if" is called for, a subject and verb immediately follow:

He acted as if he hadn't heard.

Whereas *like* simply points out a similarity between people or things, *as* makes them equivalent:

Chateau Haut Brion has a magnificent flavour, as do all the First Growths of Bordeaux.

He does as he pleases.

If you think this distinction is unnecessary, or that "like" would serve as well in these examples, consider these:

She is very forgetful, like an old person.
She is very forgetful, like an old person often is.

Both these sentences mean that her forgetfulness is *similar*, but not identical, to an old person's.

The following sentences mean that her forgetfulness is *equivalent* to an old person's.

She is as forgetful as an old person.

She is very forgetful, as an old person often is.

Finally:

While it is best to observe the distinction between *like* and *as*, it is permissible with "it looks," "feels," "tastes," "sounds" to use *like* when you mean "as if."

> George looked like he was going to be sick.
> This soup tastes like someone dropped a dead mouse into it.

LIKEWISE

In the beginning, it was "like*ways*," and that's what it meant. The original meaning and spelling still survives in "crossways" and "lengthways," although we also say crosswise and lengthwise. Clockwise describes a motion very simply and accurately and *likewise* has been around for over 200 years. Then, in the thirties, as a joke, "-wise" was tagged on to all kinds of words; by 1960, Jack Lemmon could say, "that's the way it crumbles, cookie-wise." Well, language-wise, it's all over the place today: weather-wise, transportation-wise, job-wise — you-name-it-wise.

> "Hey, Joe, how you been?"
> "Well, job-wise, not too good, but money-wise, I'm okay."

"You still looking for a job?"

"No, I got one, but it's lousy."

"Lousy pay?"

"No, money-wise it's okay, the hours are
rotten."

The example illustrates the vagueness that results from using "-wise" to mean "with respect to." "Job-wise," it turns out, communicates nothing, nor does "money-wise." The speaker could easily have said, in answer to the first question, "I got a job with lousy hours, but it pays well."

LISTS

Confusion abounds!

HORIZONTAL LISTS

A *horizontal list*, contained within a paragraph, is straightforward: it is introduced by a complete sentence that ends with a colon, and the items in the list are separated by commas; if the list items themselves contain commas, by semicolons.

The following have qualified for the team: Dunsmore, White, Wong, Alsop, Karim, Bertoluzzi.

> The team members are as follows: Dunsmore, Scott; White, Graham: Wong, Wesley; Alsop, Jim; Karim, Kazim; Bertoluzzi, Enrico.

Do not introduce a list with "are," followed by a colon, because this will make a fragment of your introductory statement. Instead, just follow "are" with your list, or reword to include "as follows," or "the following," as above:

> The members of the team are Dunsmore, White, Wong, Alsop, and Karim.

> Dunsmore, White, Wong, Alsop, and Karim are the members of the team.

VERTICAL LISTS

The method of displaying a *vertical list* varies according to the structure of the introductory statement and the listed items. The examples below are widely, though not universally, used. When you encounter variations, judge for yourself which method to follow.

Example 1: the introductory statement is a complete sentence and each list item is also a full sentence.

The characteristics of strong neighbourhoods are obvious to those who live in them:

- A range of age groups are represented, from childless couples to grandparents.
- There are sidewalks, so that neighbours can meet informally.
- There is at least one convenience store within walking distance.
- Schools are placed in the heart of the community.
- Homeowners display pride of ownership by ensuring their property is well-maintained.

Example 2: the introductory statement is a complete sentence, but each list item is not a full sentence.

Strong neighbourhoods contain the following elements:

- A range of age groups
- Sidewalks
- A convenience store
- Schools
- Pride of ownership

Example 3: the introductory statement is incomplete and therefore the items in the list must complete the sentence.

A technical report should include

- a letter of transmittal,
- an abstract,
- a table of contents,
- a list of illustrations,
- an introduction,
- appropriate graphics,
- in-text citations,
- a conclusion,
- recommendations,
- a list of references,
- a glossary, and
- appendices.

When the list items require commas, link with semicolons.

When preparing a technical report proposal, the Introduction outlines the subject matter contained in the report;

- the Body outlines the content, the methodology, and the expected accomplishments;
- the Body also includes designs, experiments,

solutions, and data analysis; and
- the Conclusions and/or Recommendations must be supported by facts or stated assumptions.

Ensure that the list items have the identical grammatical structure. (See *Parallelism*.)

NUMBERED LISTS

Number the list when the sequence is important, as in a procedure, a series of instructions or a ranking, or when you intend to refer to these items later in your text.

Horizontal

When buying a lakefront property, the most important things to check are (1) the septic tank, (2) the level of the foundation, and (3) critter damage within the subfloor.

Note: full parentheses, as above, are preferred over open parentheses: "1), 2), 3)."

Vertical

Here are the top 10 ice cream flavours:
1. Squishy Wishy
2. Triple Chocolate Fudge
   ....
10. Louisiana Vanilla

Note: If the numbered list reaches double digits (you wouldn't list more than four or five numbers in a horizontal list, so this only applies to vertical lists), ensure that the periods that follow the numbers are in line.

LITERAL/FIGURATIVE

Every word has a *literal* meaning, and many have *figurative* meanings as well. We know what to expect if we are told that someone is "fat." But a "fat contract," a "fat cat" or a "fat chance" are figurative uses.

If something is meant literally, it is to be understood for exactly what it says; if it is meant in another, less narrow, sense, as in "drop dead," then it is meant figuratively. The figurative use of language is what makes novels entertaining, while the lack of it is what makes business reports boring. (See *Simile/Metaphor.*)

MALAPROPISM/OXYMORON

Mrs. Malaprop was a character in Richard Sheridan's play *The Rivals* (1775), who, in trying to use sophisticated words, mistakenly chose words that had a similar sound but a very different meaning. Here is one of her most memorable utterances:

"If I reprehend any thing in this world, it is
the use of my oracular tongue, and a nice
derangement of epitaphs!"

The Bowery Boys' films of the 1940s made extensive
use of malapropisms, such as "I represent that
remark" for "I resent that remark," and "optimist"
for "optometrist."

When people in positions of authority make
the same sort of error, the damage to their credibility
lingers long after the laughter has subsided.

An *oxymoron* is the amusing product created
by combining contradictory terms.

Informal polls indicate that the all-time
favourite is "jumbo shrimp," with "military intel-
ligence," "mandatory option," and "pretty dirty"
close behind.

ME/MYSELF (AND I)

As a guide to the proper use of *me* and *myself,* look
at the following:

subject	object	reflexive
I	me	myself
you	you	yourself
he	him	himself
she	her	herself
it	it	itself

subject	object	reflexive
we	us	ourselves
you	you	yourselves
they	them	themselves

Notice that *me* and *myself* are not synonyms for *I*; they refer, of course, to the person, but *me* is the object form and *myself* is the reflexive (reflecting back on) form.

Notice also that there are no such words as "hisself" and "theirselves."

Now, concerning *me*:

People aren't afraid to say *me* when they're alone — "they wanted me to go" — so why are they afraid to say *me* when someone else is around? If people are referring to themselves and someone else, they tend to say, "They wanted she and I to go."

Would you say, "They wanted she to go"? Or, "They wanted I to go"?

No, you would use "her" and "me." So,

They wanted me and her to go.

Better still,

They wanted us to go.

Again:

> He lent me his car.
> He lent Fred his car.

Does it make sense now to say, "He lent Fred and I his car?"

Here's an easy way to get this straight:

If you can substitute *us* for the people involved, then you need me, him, her, etc. (The object form of the pronoun).

If you can substitute *we* for the people involved, then you need I, he, she, etc. (The subject form of the pronoun).

To return to the original example:

> They wanted she and I to go.

Is this correct? If it is, then *we* can be substituted for "she and I." Try it.

> They wanted *we* to go.

That's obviously wrong. The sentence should read, "They wanted *us* to go." Therefore, the correct pronouns are "me" and "her."

Another example:

> Me and her were given tickets to the concert.

If this is correct, then *us* can replace "me and her."
Try it.

> Us were given tickets . . .

Us is obviously wrong in this instance. *We* or "She
and I" are the correct forms.

MYSELF

People love to use *myself* when they mean *me* or *I* —
a case of self-indulgence.

Why say, "My wife and myself went to the movies"?
What's wrong with saying "My wife and I . . ."?

Similarly,

> They gave my wife and myself two fifty-pound
> sacks of oysters.

Apply the we/us rule and you will see that what is
meant is, "They gave my wife and me . . .", or, "They
gave us . . ."

Leave "myself," "yourself," etc., to perform their

intended function — reflecting actions back upon the subject.

> I did it myself.
> He hurt himself.
> (See also, *I Myself Think*.)

NEGATIVE PREFIXES

Here is a short list of troublesome words which take "in-," "im-," or "un-" as *negative prefixes*. For others, the reader is advised to consult a modern dictionary.

inadvisable	indistinguishable
inalienable	indivisible
*inalterable	inescapable
inattentive	inexcusable
incoherent	inexpensive
incomparable	infrequent
incompatible	inhuman
inconceivable	innumerable
*inconsolable	insoluble
indecipherable	insufficient
indigestible	intolerant
*indisputable	

*these are also correct with the "un-" prefix

imbalance   impassable
immaterial   impenetrable
immeasurable   imperceptive
immobile   imperfect
immodest   impractical
immoral   improbable
immovable

unacceptable   uncommunicative
unaccustomed   uncompleted
unaffected   (but "incomplete")
uncontrollable   undecided
unapproachable   undeniable
unbalanced   unexpected
unchangeable

OTHER NEGATIVE PREFIX FORMS

non-   non-violent
mal-   malevolent, malpractice
ir-   irrelevant
dis-   dissatisfied
il-   illogical
mis-   misfire

NEVER DID IT

I never took it.
I never did it.
I never saw him.

Do not use *never* as a substitute for "not" in the past tense — say instead, "I didn't take it," "I didn't do it," "I didn't see him."

However, if you mean "not ever," then use it.

I never met Princess Diana before her death.

NUMBERS

Numbers can be cardinal (1, 8, 220) or ordinal (first, second, third). Cardinal numbers denote quantity, while ordinal numbers denote a sequence.

"Numeral" denotes the symbol used to describe the number: Arabic or Roman (the latter now confined, though inconsistently, to page numbers in the front matter of books and reports, or to monuments and other artistic creations).

The following are generally accepted guidelines:

1. Spell out numbers one to nine; use Arabic numerals for quantities greater than nine.

    (Some style guides set the threshold at ten, others at twenty, still others at one hundred. As always, follow the conventional practice of your workplace.)

2. Spell out estimates expressed as a single fraction. Use numerals in mathematical contexts.

   One-third to one-half of the audience left before intermission.

   He measured the shutters at 30 x 50 centimetres.

3. Use numerals to indicate amounts of money, percent, decimals, degrees of temperature, ratios, measurements, time with p.m. and a.m., page numbers, age, address numbers, and dates. Also use numerals with "million," "billion," and "trillion."

4. If a sentence contains some numbers that should be given as numerals and others that should not, use numerals for them all.

   In the herd, Walter counted 147 antelope, 16 elephants, and 1 kangaroo!

5. Never begin a sentence with a numeral — spell out the number or re-order the sentence.

   Twenty-five (not 25) people attended.

6. When two numbers are involved, spell out the second:

   Dave began each morning by doing 25
       two-hundred-pound bench presses.
   The Kays made the mistake of inviting 10
       four-year-olds to their son's birthday
       party.

7. Two times two *is* four, not *are* four.

8. Using the word "number" can be tricky:

   The number of cars in Toronto *is* increasing.

   But:

   A number of cars were involved in the
   accident.
   (See *Collective Nouns*.)

OFF OF

If you accept "It fell off of the table," then you should accept "It fell on of the table," since using *of* is as meaningless in the first example as in the second.

The same can be said for "inside of," "underneath of," and "outside of."

PARALLELISM

> My sisters would follow me everywhere, did
> the same things, and even hung out with my
> friends.

There are three elements in this sentence, but the
third is incompatible with the other two. The construction of the sentence should be symmetrical,
imparting balance and weight.

Make the verbs parallel:

> My sisters *would follow* me everywhere, *would
> do* the same things, and *would even hang out*
> with my friends.

Or:

> My sisters *followed* me everywhere, *did* the
> same things, and even *hung out* with my
> friends.

Another example:

> I am a highly motivated self-starter, rebellious,
> and a bossy individual.

Make the characteristics parallel:

I am highly motivated, rebellious and bossy.

Parallelism is not only a matter of making the grammatical structure consistent; deliberately applied, it can also produce a compellingly balanced sentence:

> As a middle child, I wore my elder siblings' clothes until I outgrew them, and I played with their discarded toys, even if they were broken.

> He was born in Vancouver; he died in Halifax.

(See also *Lists* and *Threes.*)

PARTS OF SPEECH

O dreary phrase! But here's why it's useful to know why they exist.

Every word in English can be classified according to its function in a sentence. (Each dictionary entry immediately identifies the part of speech.) Words are merely *labels* for everything in our external and internal universe. Combined logically into sentences, they express a single *thought*. Sentences that give support to an *idea* make up a paragraph. The exploration of a *subject*, in an essay, report or book, requires many logically connected paragraphs. The list below is where it all begins.

1. **Noun**: names the class of a person, a place or a thing:

abstract:	love, hope
collective:	team, crew
common:	person, horse
proper:	Toronto

2. **Verb**: expresses action or a state of being in a particular time frame:

   She'll be living in Montreal.
   He's a smoker.
   We haven't seen them recently.

   Auxiliary verbs (ones that "help" other verbs): be, can, could, do, have, may, might, must, ought, shall, should, will, would

3. **Pronoun**: replaces a noun:

personal:	I, you, he, she, it, we, they
relative or interrogative:	who, which, what
reflexive:	myself, yourself, etc.
possessive:	mine, yours, his, hers, its, ours, theirs
demonstrative:	this, that, these, those
indefinite:	any, few, all, one

4. *Adjective*: modifies the meaning of a noun or pronoun. It answers the questions "what kind," "how many," or "which one?"

   She is a *bright, beautiful* woman.
   She drives a *bright red* car.
   She owns *four* coffee shops.

   possessive form: my, your, his, her, its,
                                        our, your, their
   demonstrative form: this, that, these, those

5. *Adverb*: modifies the meaning of a verb, adjective, or other adverbs. It answers the questions "when," "where," "why," "how," "to what degree?"

   The old man moved very *slowly*.
   Jack did *very well* on the beanstalk climb.
   They *usually* meet for coffee on Saturday
       morning.

6. *Conjunction*: a word or phrase that connects words, phrases, or clauses:

   coordinating: and, but, so, or, nor, for

       He plays tennis once a week, *but* he wishes
       he could play more.

correlative: not only, but (also), either . . . or, neither . . . nor, whether . . . or (not)

> *Either* he comes with us, *or* he stays at home.

subordinating: although, as if

> Although he plays tennis once a week, he wishes he could play more.

7. **Preposition**: shows the relation of a noun or pronoun to some other word in a sentence:

> There was an old sock that lived *in* a shoe. On sunny days they threw Frisbees *over* the house.

8. **Article**: definite: *the* — specifies a particular object:

> Please hand me *the* (specific) book.

indefinite: *a* — denotes any object of a class:

> Hand me *a* magazine (any magazine) so I can swat that fly.

PASSIVE VOICE

The *passive voice* removes the subject from active involvement — instead of controlling the action, the subject is controlled by the verb, or an agent of the verb.

> The chemicals were then placed in a beaker.
> (Active voice: Dr. Frankenstein placed the chemicals. . . .)
>
> They were led into the yard and lined up against the wall.
> (Active voice: The execution squad led them into the yard. . . .)
>
> We were told there would be jobs in this town.
> (Active voice: The governor of the state told them there would be jobs. . . .)

The passive voice is perfect for conveying objectivity, helplessness or lack of responsibility. But if you want to assert yourself, you've got to include yourself. If you don't, you'll end up with vague, disembodied statements like these:

> Writing was always difficult, but with practice it has improved.

> Many difficulties were encountered when
> looking for a job.

(See also *Vagueness/Ambiguity*.)

These statements can be made more energetic and strong by giving the subject of the sentence control of the action:

> I've always had problems with writing, but
> I've improved with practice.
> I had a lot of trouble finding a job.

PHOBIAS

We all have fears, some more natural than others, which have nothing to do with paranoia. When we speak of them, we generally use the English translation of the Greek original. "Claustrophobia" is probably the one people know best. If you suffer from "phobophobia" (fear of fear) don't bother reading the following list. You're already scared enough.

> acrophobia — heights
> ailurophobia — cats
> agoraphobia — open spaces
> astraphobia — thunderstorms
> cataphobia — falling

claustrophobia — closed spaces
hydrophobia — water
microphobia — germs
mysophobia — dirt
nyctophobia — night
pathophobia — disease
pyrophobia — fire
triskaidekaphobia — number 13
xenophobia (pronounced "zeno")
— strangers, foreigners.

Handwritten notice in the window of a Toronto purveyor of fine food:

We now sell jam's and jelleys.

Would you have the confidence to walk in and offer to trade your grammar knowledge for a basket of prepared food?

PLURALS (BROTHERS-IN-LAW)

The formation of the plural of compound nouns naturally spells trouble, since there are several nouns that could be candidates for the plural form.

Generally, the accepted rule is to add "s" to the most important word.

Thus:

> tugs of war
> holes in one
> hit-and-run-drivers
> commanders-in-chief
> attorneys general

If no word is more important than another, add "s" to the final word:

> hand-me-downs
> pick-me-ups

When the compound is written as one word, simply add "s":

> cupfuls, spoonfuls, handfuls

The rules for the formation of other tricky plurals follow.

1. Country, donkey.
   If a word ends with "y" and is preceded by a consonant, change the "y" to "i" and add the plural ending — "countries."

   If the "y" is not preceded by a consonant, add "s" — "donkeys."

2. Radio, volcano.
    If the "o" ending is preceded by a vowel, add "s"
    — radios, Cheerios, rodeos.

    If preceded by a consonant, add "es" —
    tomatoes, potatoes, volcanoes.

    Of course there are exceptions: autos, tobaccos,
    pianos, solos, banjos, sopranos, altos.

3. Nouns ending in "f" or "fe" usually change their
    ending to "ves" — knife/knives, wife/wives.
    However, some do not, and some are optional:

        scarf/scarves or scarfs
        hoof/hooves or hoofs
        roof/roofs
        belief/beliefs
        safe/safes
        dwarf/dwarfs

4. Add "'s" to letters but not to figures:

        There are four "s's" and four "i's" in
            Mississippi.
        Six 747s stood on the runway.

    When citing words, use common sense when
    applying this convention:

He uses too many "I's" in his writing.

But:

He is full of ifs, buts, and maybes.

5. Borrowed words:

analysis/analyses
appendix/appendices
basis/bases
cactus/cacti
crisis/crises
criterion/criteria
curriculum/curricula
datum/data
formula/formulae
fungus/fungi
index/indices
matrix/matrices
medium/media
memorandum/memoranda
parenthesis/parentheses
stratum/strata
thesis/theses

POSSESSIVE CASE (BOSS'S)

1. To form the possessive singular add "'s," even if the word ends in "ss":

    the cat's meow
    the witch's brew
    King Kong's mistress
    Mike Harris's golf game.
    the boss's secretary
    Ross's bad breath.

    Note that the possessive form adds an extra syllable to the word, which is why most writers prefer "Ross's" to "Ross." Since each version is pronounced in the same way, it makes sense to include the "s" that produces this extra syllable.

    "Men," "women," and "children," though plural, are also governed by this rule:

    the men's room
    women's intuition

2. To form the possessive singular of words ending in a single "s," add "'s" or the apostrophe alone ('), depending on the awkwardness of the resulting sound:

Paris's monuments.

> (The extra syllable is pronounced.)

But:

> Dickens' work (not Dickens-ez)
> Roy Rogers' horse (not Rogers-ez)
> Brahms' music (not Brahms-ez)
> Jesus' teachings (not Jesus-ez)

In the preceding examples, the addition of "'s" would unnaturally extend the final sound, so the word is left in its original state.

Obviously, there is room for interpretation here, and thus the possessive form of proper names like Eves, Hughes, and Adams appears variously as Eves's, Eves', Hughes's, Adams', etc. No rule applies in these cases; it is simply a matter of playing it by ear.

3. To form the possessive plural, add the apostrophe alone to the plural form:

> the hostesses' long hours
> the Joneses' budgie
> the Finlaysons' dogs
> the ladies' room

4. With "of"

    Of course, if possession is expressed as *x of y*, as in *House of Usher* or *friend of mine*, then no apostrophe is used. Any of the above examples could be converted to this form:

    > the long hours of the hostesses
    > the bad breath of Ross

    Be alert, however: *A painting of Picasso* and *A painting of Picasso's* do not mean the same thing.

5. Joint Possession

    > We went over to Paul and Fiona's house.

    Only the second noun takes the possessive form.

6. Compounded Possession

    > My friend's mother's estate turned out to be worthless.

    Avoid such awkwardness by rewording the sentence:

    > The estate of my friend's mother turned out to be worthless.

7. The possessive form of noun combinations is applied to the last word:

> his father-in-law's absurdities
> their daughters-in-law's dilemmas

8. Gerunds
A *gerund* is a -ing form of a verb that is sometimes used as a noun. If it is modified by a noun or pronoun, these should take the possessive form:

> "I said I would never forget him burping loudly."

If you think "him" should be "his," you're right. After all, it's *his* burping, not yours.

The rule here is that the subject of the burping must be in the possessive form in order to distinguish it from the subject (I) at the front of the sentence. But unless there is an obvious ambiguity, as there would be if a comma followed "him," most of us neglect the rule, particularly if the subject is a noun.

> I will never forget George's burping.
> (Correct)
> I will never forget George burping.
> (Acceptable)

Other examples of the same construction are:

> I didn't mind his borrowing the car.
> I don't want to complain about her going.
> We're concerned about their keeping that
> dog.

9. False? Possessives
Do you write,

> "That table's legs are too short"?

Or:

> "The legs of that table are too short"?

It is correct to write it either way, although some might insist that only living creatures are actually worthy of denoting possession. The *of* option, however, always results in a longer version.

This debate often concludes with the mystery of why, although everyone agrees that "they gave me one week's pay" is correct, not everyone agrees that applying the possessive form in the plural (as in "two weeks' pay") is worth the trouble. Many would happily write, "two weeks pay," on the grounds that it means "pay for two weeks" (descriptive) and not "two weeks *of* pay" (possessive). The guideline to follow is that the possessive form is preferred in common expressions of dollars and cents:

two weeks' pay
two cents' worth
twenty dollars' worth

However, if the first word of an expression is an adjective, it is descriptive by definition:

sales meeting
retirement savings plan
Weight Watchers diet

In others, the meaning is clearly meant to be descriptive:

aviators club (club *for*)
golfers reception (reception *for*)
professors lounge (BUT professors' employment contract)
users manual (BUT drug user's needles)

PREFIXES

A knowledge of the meaning of prefixes can aid in your understanding (or divining) the precise meaning of a word. In English, most prefixes are taken directly from Latin or Greek.

sub-	under	submarine, subversive
trans-	across	transcontinental, transplant
inter-	between	inter-office, interview
intra-	inside	intramural, intra-uterine
re-	back or again	regress, revisit
retro-	back	retro-active, retrospect
pre-	before	predestination, premeditated
ante-	before	antecedent, antebellum
post-	after	post-war, posthumous
poly-	many	polygamy, polyester
demi-	half	demi-gallon
semi-		semicircle
mono-	one	monocle, monorail
uni-		unilingual

anti-	against	anti-war, anti-climax
contra-		contraband,
		contraceptive,

ultra-	more than	ultrasonic, ultraviolet
hyper-		hyperactive, hyper-
		sensitive

extra-	above	extraordinary
super-	beyond	Superman, supercilious
supra-		

(See *Hyphenated Words.*)

PREPOSITIONS (OBLIVIOUS OF)

It is easy to forget or confuse the prepositions that follow certain words and expressions. *Oblivious of* is an example. Originally it meant "unmindful of." Today we generally say "oblivious to," and by it we mean "uncaring" or "unaware." "Of" is still the correct preposition, but "to" is acceptable. Other similarly confusing companion prepositions follow:

Accompanied *with* things; accompanied
   by people.
Concur *in* an action or decision; concur
   with people.
Acquiesce *to*.
Adhere *to*; an adherence *of*.

Admit (it is unnecessary to add "to").

Agree *with* a view; agree *to* an action.

Aim *at*, not *for*.

Speak *on* someone's behalf (stand in for him); speak *in* someone's behalf (speak in his interest).

Culminate *in*.

Dismayed *with*.

Identical *with*.

Instil *in*.

In regard *to* (*as* regards, but never *regards*).

(See *Regardless/Irregardless*.)

RUN-ON SENTENCES

A sentence will end sooner or later, and the reader must know that it's ended. Complete sentence units can be linked by semicolons and words like "and" or "but" or "because," and they can be ended with a period, a question mark or an exclamation mark. When these links and stops are not used and the writer plunges ahead from one sentence unit to the next, run-on sentences like these are created:

It was a cold day we stayed in.

We found a hotel the next day we went shopping.

Never use a comma to do the work of a semicolon, a period, or a necessary linking word.

> It was a cold day, we stayed in.
> We found a hotel, the next day we went
>   shopping.

It is relatively easy to correct a run-on sentence: read it carefully and decide where it should be linked or ended. Usually there are a number of choices available, depending on how the writer would like the sentence to read:

> It was a cold day. We stayed in.
> It was a cold day; we stayed in.
> It was a cold day, and (so) we stayed in.

> We found a hotel. The next day we went
>   shopping.
> We found a hotel, and the next day . . .
> We found a hotel the next day, and then
>   we went . . .

SENTENCE FRAGMENTS

Sentence fragments are incomplete sentences. In dialogue ("Maybe"), in commands ("Stop!"), or exclamations ("Oh my gosh!"), fragments are quite acceptable. After all, that's often the way we speak. Sentence fragments are the reverse of run-ons — they end too soon:

> I got my grade 12. Which was the last grade I took.
> I gave them to my husband. Since he is a student.
> Caesar escaped to Egypt; where he met Cleopatra.
> We went to all kinds of places. Trying to find the right one.
> He had a few rules. The first being unacceptable.

These can be corrected as follows:

> I got my grade 12, which was the last grade I took.
> I gave them to my husband, since he is a student.
> Caesar escaped to Egypt, where he met Cleopatra.
> We went to all kinds of places, trying to find the right one.
> His first rule was unacceptable.

SIMILE/METAPHOR

These are the primary devices for comparison and description. A *simile* (*sim*-ill-ee) is used to compare one thing to another, suggesting a similarity, while a *metaphor* is a single or sustained image applied outside its normal context, as implied in the expression, "Golf is a metaphor for life." Both are known as figures of speech. The first three of the following are examples of similes, the last three examples are metaphors.

> Uncle Fred eats like a horse.
> When we got home the house was as cold
>   as ice.
> Generally, he behaved like a child, and
>   certainly was as demanding.

> He was a great walrus of a man.
> "Drop-kick me Jesus through the goalposts of
>   life" is a famous line from a forgotten song.
> In the winter of his days he withdrew into his
>   books and his brandy.

(See *Like/As*.)

STILL/YET

When used as time references, they are not truly synonyms and today *yet* is rarely used in the affirmative:

> Horace still has his cold, but I haven't gotten
> it yet.
>
> Does he still have that old car? Hasn't he sold
> it yet?

SUBJECT-PRONOUN AGREEMENT (EVERYONE KNOWS HIS/HER, THEIR)

A pronoun must agree with the word it stands for. Because *everyone* is singular, its pronoun reference must also be singular. The following examples illustrate common errors:

> She was one of those women who never
> revealed *their* (her) age.
>
> A person (People) just can't take whatever
> *they* want.
>
> The athlete is in a class by *themselves*
> (herself).

The above mistakes are caused by an inconsistency in number between subject and pronoun reference.

When the pronoun is singular, the gender is either female or male. In one of the above examples, the gender is specified. However, when it is unknown, the practice today is to change the subject (and matching pronoun) to the plural:

By opening night, everyone knows his/her role.
(By opening night, all actors knew their roles.)

This has largely replaced the use of "his/her" (and its variants), which was always cumbersome, especially when repeated throughout a text.

Some writers, particularly in the humanities, alternate the masculine and feminine reference from paragraph to paragraph. If you encounter this approach, you might be surprised at how quickly you adapt to it. (See *Inclusive Language* for a related discussion.)

Beyond such judgment calls, here are some rules:

1. The following words always take a singular verb and a singular pronoun: *someone, somebody, everybody, everyone, something, everything, nothing, anyone, anybody, no one, nobody, person, man, woman, one, each, either, neither.*

    Everybody in the company is welcome to attend.

2. With collective nouns such as team, group, council, etc. (see *Collective Nouns*) use a singular pronoun when the group is seen as a whole, a plural pronoun when it is seen as a collection of individuals:

The captain instructed the crew to wear
their whites for the admiral's
inspection.
The admiral thought it was the finest crew
he'd seen.

3.   With multiple subjects joined by "either . . . or,"
or "neither . . . nor," the pronoun agrees with
the subject that is closest to it:

Either John or the boys *were* going to do it.
Neither the children nor their mother *has*
any clothes.

(See *Either. . . or/Neither . . . nor.*)

SUBJUNCTIVE MOOD (IF I WERE)

Smith was shot with a .38 calibre pistol. "It was
a through and through wound," Detective
Franks said, making it impossible to tell if he
were shot in the front or the back of the head.

Whoever wrote this was aware that "were" replaces
"was" after "if" in certain instances — but not, as it
happens, in this one. "Were" should be "had been"
or "was."

The rule for determining this is simple: when

expressing contemporary unreality or a desire that is contrary to fact, "were" is used for all persons of the verb "to be."

Thus:

> If I were you, I'd get a haircut.
> I wish I were you.

In both of these examples, a hypothetical situation is expressed; in the Smith example, the situation is fact. A man *was* shot and the wound *was* visible.

> In, "If I were you I'd get a haircut," I'm not
> you, and never can be. The unreality is clear.

However, in instances not involving the substitution of people, the degree of unreality is usually a matter of opinion. For instance, in the sentence "I wish I weren't so dumb" (but I am, alas), the fact is much stronger than the wish, and it is more natural to say, "I wish I wasn't so dumb." This jostling of reality with expressed unreality is especially tricky with "as if." Although, "He looked as if he were going to throw up" is the correct form (since he didn't throw up) the reality would undoubtedly have been strong enough to warrant saying "as if he *was* going to throw up."

One's own dreams and wishes, of course, are unreal by definition, and in these instances "were" must be used. Perhaps you are familiar with these fanciful longings:

> If I *were* a carpenter, and you were a lady ...
> I wish I *were* a Kellogg's cornflake ...

THESE KIND OF THINGS

Make each word plural, or each word singular.

> This/that kind of thing.
> These/those kinds of things.

THREES

You're giving examples to illustrate some great insight you've reached. The first two trip off your tongue and you're into the third — and all of a sudden it doesn't come and you stutter ... and pause ... and reword your sentence for two examples only. What led you to attempt a third example when none was there?

This is the phenomenon of *threes*, which describes the tendency of the human mind to group examples and supporting points in grammatically identical sequences of three. You could say that this is the ultimate expression of *parallelism*.

Speeches very consciously employ this device. It establishes a cadence that, persuasive in the consistency of its pattern, leads to a satisfying and harmonious conclusion:

> In a whirlwind of change, and hope, and peril, our faith is sure, our resolve is firm, and our union is strong.

> These good works deserve our praise, our personal support, and our assistance.

("Threesome," of course, has an entirely different meaning.)

TITLES

Book titles and the names of operas, plays, musicals, and films are written in italics. Works within works are placed within quotation marks. The words "the" and "and" are usually not capitalized unless they are the first word of the title or an integral part of it.

> William Zinsser's *On Writing Well* is a superb book.
> Inspector Clouseau, played by Peter Sellers in *The Pink Panther*, is an incompetent klutz.
> "Get me to the Church on Time" is a song from the musical, *My Fair Lady*.

"Going Away" is the best poem in the
collection, *Coming Back.*

(See *Quotation Marks.*)

UNWITTING SHIFTS

Inappropriate or inaccurate *shifts* in subject, time, and structure will confuse the reader. Careful proofreading, especially out loud, usually makes such errors glaringly obvious.

1. Shift of subject

    If *you* learned the rules, *anyone* could
    play poker.

    The subjects must be consistent: "you/you," or "Once the rules are learned, anyone . . ." This shift is explained more fully under *Subject-Pronoun Agreement.*

2. Shift of voice

    We went (active voice) shopping and some
    things *were purchased* (passive voice).

    George studied (active voice) for six years
    and *was* finally *graduated* (passive voice).

These sentences should read:

> We went shopping and (we) purchased
> some things.

> George studied for six years and (he)
> finally graduated.

When the subject is repeated, as in these examples, never change from the active voice to the passive, and vice versa. Say, "I *did this* and I *did this*," not "I *did this* and this *was done* by me."

3. Shift in tense

> I have taken a reading course when I found
> out my speed is slow.

In this extreme example the writer uses three tenses — the present perfect, the past, and the present.

But the reference is to something that took place in the past; thus, the simple past tense is the correct choice:

> I *took* a reading course when I *found out*
> my reading *was* slow.

In a long sentence or paragraph, it is often very easy to switch tenses (usually past-present-past) without realizing it. The error can only be discovered by careful proofreading, and corrected by placing all the subject verbs in the same time frame. This is especially necessary when paraphrasing a written passage. (See *Indirect/Direct Speech*.)

4. Shifts in structure:

    (a) My main difficulties are sentence structure and using the correct words.

    (b) Caesar was intending to meet Pompey's army and destroying it.

    (c) The author shows us how these people were dealt with, and also to show that a communication gap existed.

    Corrections:

    (a) My main difficulties are structure and vocabulary.

    The writer identifies two difficulties; if the first is expressed by a noun, so should the second.

(b) He was intending to meet and destroy
     Pompey's army.

The writer confuses what "destroy" is related to.
Caesar was intending two things: (1) to meet
Pompey's army and (2) to destroy it.

(c) He shows us how these people were
     dealt with, and he also shows us that a
     communication gap existed.

Again, the two clauses must be grammatically
symmetrical.

Comma Mania

*Elderly people who have slow reflexes shouldn't be
allowed to drive.*

The sentence could stand as it is but would
have a very different meaning with the correct
placement of two commas.

How would this change the meaning?
(See *Who/Which/That* p. 95)

VAGUENESS/AMBIGUITY

Make sure that your reader knows whom and what you are talking about. Ensure that the subject is clear, the verb is precise, and the pronoun references (if any) are obvious:

> There were a lot of memories.

(Whose memories?)

> Having slept soundly, we took the dog for a walk.

(Who slept?)

> This report looks into bridge-building techniques.

(Describes, examines, compares, evaluates?)

> His mother divorced at his birth and never told him about his father. Many years later, she revealed she regretted it.

(What does "it" relate to? The divorce, the silence, the birth, all of them?)

Finally, sometimes it is really difficult to figure out how to say what you mean. Keep testing versions by putting yourself in the place of the reader. Don't give up and leave a sloppy sentence!

Notice how the first three versions of this sentence are ambiguous:

> She can't keep her husbands straight.
> She mixes up her husbands.
> She confuses her husbands.

Any of the following clears the ambiguity:

> She confuses one husband with the next.
> All her husbands look the same.
> She can't tell her husbands apart.

WHO/WHICH/THAT

As relative pronouns, these are linking words that introduce information relevant to the subject or object of a sentence. This information is classified as being either essential to understanding the full meaning of the sentence, or non-essential, meaning that the information could be removed without affecting the meaning. This distinction dictates whether commas are used.

The example displayed in one of the sidebars illustrates this difference:

Elderly people *who have slow reflexes* shouldn't be allowed to drive.

This means that *only* those with slow reflexes should not drive. In other words, "Elderly people who have slow reflexes" is the full subject of the sentence and is therefore essential information.

However, if we mean that *all* elderly people have slow reflexes and therefore none should be allowed to drive, the clause "who have slow reflexes" becomes non-essential information.

Elderly people, *who have slow reflexes*, shouldn't be allowed to drive.

The commas separate the non-essential information, assisting the reader to connect the subject and the verb.

Another example:

"The two pedestrians who were injured were taken to Sunnybrook Hospital."

This sentence means that there were more than two pedestrians in total. If there were only two, then commas would be needed to indicate the non-essential information.

Which introduces clauses of non-essential information only:

The CN Tower, *which* was once the tallest structure in the world, will last forever.

That introduces clauses of essential information only:

There's the house that burned down.

Commas should not be used around information that is essential to the meaning of the sentence.

That can also be used to introduce essential information about a person who is remote from you or whose name you do not know:

There's the cop that gave me the ticket.
He's the guy that lost the wallet.

In summary:

Do not use commas for clauses that contain essential information.

Use commas for clauses that contain non-essential information.

Who can introduce both types of clause.

Which introduces only clauses that contain non-essential information.

That introduces only clauses that contain essential information.

"Whom Do You Believe?"
asked the newspaper headline.
Can you explain why this is a correct use of
"whom"?   (See *Who/Whom* p. 97)

"As far as I'm concerned, the word 'whom' is a
word that was invented to make everyone
sound like a butler."

— CALVIN TRILLIN (1935–)

WHO/WHOM

Whom is so little heard today that its use can seem pompous and affected, but its correct use is still expected in writing. *Whom* stands for an object noun; *who* stands for a subject noun:

Whom did you see last night?
We saw *George.*

Who called?
Alice called.

Whom is also used when the object pronoun is preceded by a preposition:

> On whom can we depend?
> Whom can we depend on?
> To whom do we owe the money?

If you can replace the person in question with "he" or "she" or "they," then *who* is correct. If "him," "her," or "them" is suitable, then *whom* is the correct choice.

(See *Me/Myself (And I)* for a similar explanation.)

WILL/SHALL

Will is used to express the future tense, with the implication of commitment to a stated action.

For example, a questioner inquires about willingness:

> "Will you take out the garbage?"

The responder states intention:

> "Yes, I will."
> "No, I won't."

In North American usage, *shall* is rarely used to express the future, except as a playful substitution for *will*:

> We shall see.

However, *shall* is commonly used to convey an offer or suggestion, as in "Shall we go?" and "Shall I get some coffee?" and its use in directing policy or procedure persists:

> When academic cheating is alleged, the Dean shall convene a meeting with the student and the professor.

> "I apologize for the long letter. I didn't have time to shorten it."
> — PLINY THE YOUNGER (A.D. 62–113)

WORD INFLATION

Make every word count for something. If your message is stuffed with filler, it will be unclear. The simplest, most accurate word or phrase is always the best choice.

There are 262 words in the left hand column, 88 in the right. Using the fillers on the left would make your message 3 times longer and 3 times less effective!

HIGH CARB PHRASES
Several words are used when one will do.

a large number	many
at a rapid rate	rapidly
at all times	always
at that point in time	then
at the present time	now, today
at the rate of	20% year, 80 km per hour
at this point in time	now
aware of the fact that	aware that
by means of (fiscal restraint)	by (saving)
despite the fact that	despite
due to the fact that	because
for the purpose of	to (verb)
for the simple reason that	because
in the course of	during
in the event that	if
in the near future	soon, next week, etc.
on a personal basis	I/me
personally, I believe	I believe
rior to	before
regardless of the fact that	regardless, in spite of

subsequent to	after
the majority of	most
until such time as	until
	(time reference)

NOUN GRAFTING

A perfectly good verb is replaced by its noun form, which requires another verb to make it do the work of the original verb. (So much for conciseness!)

come to a conclusion	conclude
conduct an inspection of	inspect
conduct an investigation of	investigate
conduct a study of	study
conduct a test of	test
display a tendency to	tend to
give a summary of	summarize
give consideration to	consider
give instruction to	instruct
have a discussion about	discuss
have compliance with	comply
have the effect of causing	cause
have the ability to	can, is able
have the intention of	intend
hold a meeting	meet
I am of the belief that	I believe
in need of	need, require
is in conflict with	conflict with
make a decision	decide

make a recommendation	recommend
provide an explanation of	explain
provide a description of	describe
take action	act

Here is a Defense Department policy directive submitted to President Roosevelt shortly after the bombing of Pearl Harbor:

"Such preparations shall be made as will completely obscure all Federal buildings and non-Federal buildings occupied by the Federal Government during an air raid for any period of time from visibility by reason of internal or external illumination. Such obscuration may be obtained either by blackout construction or by termination of the illumination. This will, of course, require that in building areas in which production must continue during the blackout, construction must be provided that internal illumination may continue. Other areas, whether or not occupied by personnel, may be obscured by terminating the illumination."

Roosevelt's rewording:

"Tell them that in buildings where they have to keep the work going, put something across the window. In buildings where they can afford to stop work for a while, turn out the lights."

OVERKILL
A redundant qualifier is added to the noun or verb. (This is *really* pointless!)

cancel out	cancel
completely eliminate	eliminate
consensus of opinion	consensus
co-operate together	co-operate
dead corpse	corpse
dig in the ground	dig
disappear from view	disappear
end result	result
enter into	enter
final conclusion	conclusion
free gift	gift
important essentials	essentials
in this world today	today
mental awareness	awareness
mutual co-operation	co-operation

natural ecosystem	ecosystem
natural vegetation	vegetation
new innovation	innovation
rain shower activity	rain
resulting effect	effect
safety precaution	precaution
snow flurry activity	snow
visual distraction	distraction

Check out these winners:

afternoon hours	afternoon
attractive in appearance	attractive
audible to the ears	audible
blue in colour	colour
cheaper in cost	cheaper
few in number	few
in the morning period	in the morning
month of August	August
round in shape	round
rose $200 in price	rose $200
small in size	small
young in age	young

PUNCTUATION

Spoken language is punctuated by variations in pitch, emphasis, and speed. Gestures and facial expressions — body language — are also punctuation devices. In writing, this same sort of expressiveness can only be conveyed by the use of punctuation symbols. Certain conventions govern their use, but a great deal of flexibility is allowed. Punctuation is only wrong when it obscures or distorts the intended meaning. Some writers try to dress up their sentences by sprinkling commas here and there. This approach is worse than avoiding punctuation altogether. Why? Because the effective use of punctuation in a sentence enables the reader to quickly assess the relationship of the parts to the whole and to separate the essential from the non-essential information. A sentence lacking necessary punctuation is as uninviting as a forest without a path: signposts are needed to guide the way.

The following examples illustrate how the use of different punctuation symbols can affect the meaning of a sentence.

The back door was wide open, and the chain lock had been cut through.
(Two things are observed without emphasizing the relationship between them.)

The back door was wide open: the chain lock had been cut through.
(Each observation is more emphatic, and a relationship is suggested.)

The back door was wide open. The chain lock had been cut through.
(The observations are distinctly separate, suggesting an interval between the first and the second — perhaps the time it has taken the observer to realize the connection between them.)

The back door was wide open — the chain lock had been cut through.
(The dash leads our eyes from the first observation to the second, in much the same way as the observer's eyes moved from door to chain.)

All of these sentences are correct and they illustrate that punctuation is as much a guide to the eye as it is to the ear.

Here is another example of how a single sentence can be expressed in different ways, with the appropriate punctuation:

> He plays tennis once a week. He wishes he could play more.

> He plays tennis once a week, but he wishes he could play more.

> He plays tennis once a week but wishes he could play more.

> He plays tennis once a week; he wishes he could play more.

> He plays tennis once a week; however, he wishes he could play more.

> He plays tennis once a week. However, he wishes he could play more.

> Although he plays tennis once a week, he wishes he could play more.

The symbols can be classified as follows:

1. To stop: period, question mark, exclamation point.

2. To separate: comma, semicolon.

3. To break: dash, ellipsis points.

4. To quote: quotation marks.

5. To include: parentheses, brackets.

6. To introduce: colon.

For explanations and examples of the use of these, locate them under separate listings. (Ellipsis points are included under *Quoting.*)

Caution: *never* place a punctuation symbol at the beginning of a line
    , like this.

Comma Quiz
Are commas required in the following?
If so, where?
1. Although I like Martha Stewart is my favourite cousin.
2. Mary Dawson who replaced Betty Szo yesterday painted a picture of unethical conduct throughout the organization.

(See *Comma* p. 111)

A professor of English once tried to impress American poet Robert Frost with the following: "Mr. Frost, did you know that 'sugar' is the only word in the English language that begins with 'su' and is pronounced 'shu'?"

Frost paused for a moment. "_____," he said.

What was his clever one-word reply?
(See p. 122)

BRACKETS

In a quotation, square brackets enclose information that did not appear in the original. For example, in a book about hockey, the writer might be discussing Maurice (the Rocket) Richard, who had two brothers. After establishing whom he is talking about, the writer might refer to him simply as "Richard." But if that sentence were quoted, Richard's first name would be added so that the reader knows which Richard is meant.

He is convinced that "[Maurice] Richard was the most explosive goal scorer of all time."

Brackets are also used to insert logical connectives within a fragmented quotation:

The President told his audience that "we are open to dialogue . . . [but] we will not give in to terrorists."

Angle brackets (< >) are placed before or after a figure to signify "less than" or "greater than." They are not quotation marks, but mathematical symbols.

However, they are also used to enclose a web address when applying the MLA style. (See *Documenting Sources*, "Works Cited.")

COLON

The colon can introduce a statement, a list, or a quotation:

> Let me make this clear: there will be no moustaches or beards on this team.
> This is how the lottery winners have spent their money: Farnsworth bought a castle in the sky; Cuttlesby purchased a pipe dream; Rigby hitched a ride on a rainbow.
> Snowed under by ex-wives and girlfriends, Suttcliffe recalled the immortal line of Christopher Dobbs: "They are the millstones around my albatross."

COMMA

The comma is a separator. It calls for a very brief pause and helps sort out bunched-up information. Though rather insignificant in appearance, and often carelessly used to spice up the look of a sentence, a missing or misplaced comma can seriously confuse the reader. Let's start with the answers to the Comma Quiz on page 108:

> Although I like Martha, Stewart is my favourite cousin.

(The sentence begins with *although*, so we know that there will be two subjects — in this case, Martha *and* Stewart.)

> When in discussion, do you encourage others to voice an opinion?

> When in discussion do you encourage others to voice an opinion?

(Both of these are correct: the first means "do you encourage others at all when you are in discussion?" and the second means "at what point in the discussion do you encourage others?")

> Mary Dawson, who replaced Betty Szo yesterday, painted a picture of unethical conduct throughout the organization.

> Mary Dawson, who replaced Betty Szo,
> yesterday painted a picture of unethical
> conduct throughout the organization.

(As you can see, this one depends on the exact relationship of "yesterday" to the rest of the sentence. Both versions are correct.)

> When a community complains about
> cloudiness in the water pressure can be
> exerted to replace the system immediately.

(You probably read to the word "pressure" before you realized that the first part of the sentence ends with "water" and the second part begins with "pressure." As with the first example, a comma between the two prevents the confusion.)

The comma is used in many ways, but here are the most common uses:

1. To separate names, words, or phrases in a series:

> Ralph, Roland, and June chatted over
> chicken livers and Cokes.
> June was tall, blond, and extremely
> friendly.

(Use of the second comma depends on how different the items are and if you wish to emphasize this difference.)

Ralph worked at Riley's Tropical Fish,
Roland at Elm Used Furniture, and June
at Loretta's Lunch.

2. Before *and, but, so, yet, or*, and *nor* when they
join two complete sentences:

Ralph and Roland worked across from
    Loretta's, so June served them at
    breakfast, lunch, and coffee breaks.
A customer had returned a Blue Angel, but
    Ralph was unconcerned.
The fish was in a baggie tacked to the door,
    and there was a note attached.

3. To separate a word or group of words that
provides additional information about a person
or a thing:

Riley, the owner, investigated the incident.
Riley, who had been vacationing in Wawa,
    rushed home to investigate.
Riley, the owner, who had been
    vacationing in Wawa, rushed home.

The note, which demanded that a forty-
pound lake trout be left in the alley,
was printed in a bold hand.

4. To separate *of course*, *however*, *incidentally*, *by the way*, etc., when they begin a sentence:

> Incidentally, there was a phone number on the note.
> By the way, the number was June's.
> Roland, of course, was responsible.

5. To separate days from years:

> The date on the note was February 10, 1964.

6. To separate places from bigger places:

> Ralph's mother phoned from Phoenix, Arizona, with more news about her health.

Finally, here are some examples of sentences that have been ruined by misplaced commas. In each example, the phrase (begun by *who*, *that*, and *what*) cannot be separated from the rest of the sentence. The unnecessary break causes the sentence's meaning to become confused:

> Roland was a prankster who was, suffering serious business losses.

> Everyone felt so sorry for June that, they
>   left huge tips for a week.
> No one had a clue, what the Blue Angel
>   caper meant.

(See also *Who/Which/That*.)

DASH

The dash is an effective and emphatic way to inter-ject or tag on information.

It sets off examples:

> He had a number of jobs — shepherd, rink
> attendant, yo-yo stringer — but had never
> been content with any of them.

It can emphasize additional information:

> Although Snipper got a raise — $44 a month
> — he still couldn't afford the trip to Moose
> Factory.

It can tag on a conclusion:

> The Americans will never dominate the hockey
> puck industry — Canada would never allow it.

Dashes, commas, and parentheses (round brackets) all can be used to enclose non-essential informa-tion, each with a different effect:

Mrs. Grundy, my former grade one teacher,
     just won $20 million.
(The commas indicate that you are neutral
about the information they enclose.)

Mrs. Grundy (my former grade one teacher)
     just won $20 million.
(The parentheses include the information
almost as an afterthought, by removing it
from the body of the sentence.)

Mrs. Grundy — my former grade one teacher
     — just won $20 million.
(The dashes interrupt the sentence to
emphasize the information.)

In these uses, commas are silent, parentheses
whisper, and dashes shout.

A hyphen is not the same thing as a dash, nor as long.
A hyphen connects two words to form a compound
word, such as "long-winded"; a dash separates words
or phrases within a sentence — like that.
(See *Hyphenated Words.*)

EXCLAMATION POINT

The only caution here is not to overdo it. It signals
exclamations of surprise, astonishment, urgency, etc.

Save it for those times when it's absolutely necessary!

> It's the Martians!
> Mom! Granddad let the air out of all his tires!

PARENTHESES

Parentheses enclose information that is relevant to the sentence but not essential to it.

This information might:

1. Refer the reader to a passage elsewhere in a book.

   > And thus, with a steel bar driven through his skull, Phineas Gage received the world's first recognized lobotomy (see Bizarre Behaviour, p. 315).

2. Supply a useful fact.
   > Trigger (Roy Rogers' golden palomino) was the smartest horse who ever lived.

3. Ask a question.
   > Hector McCann (who remembers him now?) was World Tiddlywink Champion through the thirties.

4. Give an opinion.
    > The Slobs (and that is what they are) grossed out everybody last night at the Heavy Number.

> "If one waits for the right time to come before writing, the right time never comes."
> — JAMES RUSSELL LOWELL (1819–1891)

PERIOD

The period, or full stop, is used:

1. To end a sentence that does not require a question mark or an exclamation mark.
    > Around the rugged rock the ragged rascal ran.

2. At the end of most abbreviations.
    > First it was his back, then his neck and nose, etc., etc.

Punctuation immediately following an abbreviation is normal except for the period, which is not repeated.

(See *Latin Abbreviations*.)

QUESTION MARK

1. At the end of a direct question:

    "When is Daddy coming back from space?"

2. At the end of a statement that asks for confirmation or registers surprise:

    You'll be there? (Won't you?)
    She was with the Hell's Angels last night?

3. Within parentheses to indicate uncertainty:

    Chaucer (1340?–1400) described a cook with a runny nose and sores on his face.

    Remember when you've asked a question. It's sometimes easy to forget, especially in sentences like these:

    He can do what he likes, but with what effect.
    What can I do when he refuses to see a doctor about his fused toes.
    Why don't they do something if they know all the answers.

Each of these sentences asks a question and must end with a question mark.

"Your a very poor communicator," wrote the supervisor to the employee.
(See *Spelling and Common Confusions* p. 213)

QUOTATION MARKS

There is a significant difference between British and North American usage; namely, the British way is the opposite of ours. Where we use full quotation marks, they use single; where we use single, they use full. If you don't believe such a thing to be possible, compare a book printed in Britain with one published in Canada or the United States. The British practice leaves the page — particularly a page of dialogue — less cluttered, and readers might prefer it for that reason. But you're in North America and you're stuck with the North American way. Here it is.

Full (" ") quotation marks are used:

1. To indicate a phrase or passage spoken or written by someone other than the writer (unless the writer is self-quoting).

    Dead silence followed Sidley's shout, "I deny the allegation and defy the allegator!"

2. When naming works of art or any published work included in another work (a short story, for instance, or a magazine article). (See *Titles*.)

> Freddie's aunt smiles like the "Mona Lisa."
> Fogle's famous story, "Me," appears in his collection, *Woe is Me*, 1928.

Book titles and the names of operas, plays, musicals and films are set in italics.

3. When referring to a particular word or saying:

> "Groovy" in the sixties became "outrageous" in the seventies, "insane" in the eighties, "wicked" in the nineties, and "awesome" in whatever we call today.

> If you said "groovy" today, people would think you were out of your tree.

4. As a replacement for "so-called," to indicate sarcasm or non-acceptance of the usual meaning:

> Uncle Perry is always being taken advantage of by his "friends" down at the Legion.

Single (' ') quotation marks are used to indicate a quotation within a quotation:

> An excited woman once rushed up to Robert Frost and exclaimed, "Mr. Frost, did you know that 'sugar' is the only word in the English language that begins with 'su' but is pronounced 'shu?'" Frost paused for a moment. "Sure," he said.

Rules for the placement of punctuation when quoting:

1. Periods and commas at the end of quoted material are placed inside the quotation marks:

   > "If I had to do it over again," said Sir Budge, "I'd do it as a giant squid."

2. Colons and semicolons are placed outside the quotation marks:

   > Sir Cedric speculated on the development of physics "had Newton been struck on the head by a coconut instead of an apple": we might still be awaiting a "more fortunate Newton," he concluded.

3. Question marks and exclamation points are placed inside the quotation marks if they are part of the quotation, outside if they are not:

> "Are you still behind me, Ruth?" shouted Howard, as he sped ruthlessly through the night.

> Even more baffling was his statement, "People who live in stone houses shouldn't throw glass"!

The Globe and Mail, July 1, 2004

"Being a single mother makes it difficult to find a mate — even when you're actress Nicole Kidman. 'I'm hoping to meet someone and be happy with them. But that's not as easy as it sounds.'"

How many people does Nicole hope to meet? (See *Subject-Pronoun Agreement* p. 83)

QUOTING

Quotations illustrate, emphasize or expand the point being made, and they should be chosen carefully and used sparingly. In academic papers, quotations support and illustrate your argument — they are your evidence. The mechanics of quoting follow.

RUN-IN QUOTATIONS

This method is used for short quotations (phrases or several lines) that are best integrated into the text, without interrupting its rhythm.

> During that summer, Miss Hoymee tells us, "all sorts of strange creatures" came calling; one was Bertie Tweed, "a preposterous toad," who was destined to become "the soul, the fire, the light of my life. . . ."

A comma is used to introduce a run-in quotation.

A colon may be used to introduce (within the text) a short quotation that illustrates a specific point:

> The journey was long and tedious: "We had despaired of ever reaching dear England."

BLOCK QUOTATIONS

As the term suggests, these are longer passages (more than three lines is suggested, but there is no consistent agreement on length) and they are set off from the main text to emphasize their importance. They are introduced with a colon, indented from the left margin, and no quotation marks are used.

They left the muddy town of York on
November 10, and Foster resumed his diary:

> All are mighty glad to be gone from that
> dang-blasted mudhole. Yet the populace,
> ridiculously haughty in their besmirched
> clothing and lumpen shoes, is mightily
> pleased with all around them, though the
> shops be empty of civilized goods and the
> countryside nothing but forest and rocks.
> It is astonishing that anyone could settle
> in such a backwater.

QUOTING VERSE

Use a slash (/) to indicate the end of a verse line. Line,
act or scene references can be given in parentheses
at the end of the quotation. For longer quotations,
use block quotation format.

> Everyone, of course, remembers the Duchess's
> retort: "Where have you been/Silly boy, silly
> boy/What sport/Could please your peasant
> taste?" (3, ii)

> James McIntyre, "The Cheese Poet," was best
> known for his poem, "Ode on the Mammoth
> Cheese (Weighing over 7000 pounds)." Here
> are the first two stanzas of this hilariously
> dreadful six-stanza poem:

We have seen thee, queen of cheese,
Lying quietly at your ease,
Gently fanned by evening breeze
Thy fair form no flies dare seize.

All gaily dressed soon you'll go
To the great Provincial show
To be admired by many a beau
In the city of Toronto.

BROKEN QUOTATIONS

To indicate a break in quoted material, ellipsis points are used, followed by a period if the break continues to the end of the sentence being quoted:

In one of his letters he notes that, "My dear Virginia . . . has run off to join the circus."

And, later on, "I fear the rest of this kooky family will join her. . . ."
(Note that a period follows the ellipsis points in this sentence.)

INTEGRATING QUOTATIONS

Quotations must be integrated with the text so that they seem to be a natural part of it. Quotations can't be left hanging or drifting; their relevance must be instantly obvious to the reader. Decide why you've selected a particular quotation and then make sure you pass this on to the reader. Usually a quotation illustrates some-thing — make clear what you think it illustrates.

Quotations must also be integrated with the structure of your sentences, so that the resulting sentence containing the quotation is readable and grammatically sound. Some examples follow:

Original:

I was the only paying guest at the Hotel Nacional at that time — all fidelistas with beards and armed to the teeth, living like kings — and cane-cutter peasants.

Quotation:

The Hotel Nacional, where he was staying as the only paying guest, was "[full of] fidelistas with beards . . . armed to the teeth, living like kings. . . ."

Original:

They thought I was a Russian, and always gave me the right of way in the elevator — I kept my mouth shut.

Quotation:

They showed him respect because, "they thought I was a Russian," and he kept silent so as not to give himself away.

You will notice in the first example that "full of" has been placed inside brackets. Insertions are sometimes necessary to retain the original sense of the material. (See *Brackets*.)

SEMICOLON

1. The semicolon can replace a period or a connecting word like "and," (others are "but," "so," "yet," "or," and "nor") as long as the sentence on each side of it is complete, meaning that each has a subject and a verb:

> Jake plays tennis once a week. He wishes he could play more.
> Jake plays tennis once a week, but he wishes he could play more.
> Jake plays tennis once a week; he wishes he could play more.

The semicolon signals, but does not specify, a relationship between the two sentences that it connects. This can impart subtlety to the relationship, not to mention an alternative to repetitively using "and" and "but," etc.

Here's a sentence whose meaning is perfectly suited to the use of the semicolon:

He was born in Vancouver; he died in Halifax.

The semicolon points to the contrast of birth and death, west and east, without intruding. Using "and" instead would result in a less satisfying sentence. Do you agree?

Here are two more examples:

The fuselage of the Concorde was built by France; Britain built the engines and wings.

They clung to the overturned boat all day; by nightfall their number had been reduced by two.

When used as connectors, "however" and "therefore" require the use of the semicolon, which underlines the more emphatic role they play compared with their shorter equivalents, "but" and "so."

Thus:

She loves cats, but she doesn't like dogs.
She loves cats; however, she doesn't like dogs.

If you write, "She loves cats, however she doesn't like dogs," you are wasting the more emphatic contrast that the use of "however" delivers.

2. In addition to "however" and "therefore," the semicolon is used before other transition words and phrases, such as "nevertheless," "in fact," "besides," "consequently," "of course," "on the contrary," etc.:

    > When Albert's weight reached 170 kg, Ruth began to worry; in fact, she felt nervous when he was feeding nearby.

    > Procrastinators dawdle and yawn, stretch and cry out in frustration; consequently, they spend most of their life in pajamas.

3. The semicolon is also the conventional separator for complex lists that contain commas:

    > So far, the candidates are Richard Shaw, 27 Soho St., Toronto; Robert Loblaw, 35 Albany Cres., Port Credit; Anne Gormly, 1626 Pine Ridge Ave., Toronto.

SLASH

The forward slash is a versatile symbol:

1. It can join two time periods:

    He spent the summer in Dawson City, recalling the golden days of '97/'98.

2. It can replace "per," when signifying the rate at which some action takes place:

    They flew down the road at 160 *km/hr.*

3. It can signify an alternative:

    We can meet at *my/your* house.
    (Note that this is really just shorthand for using "or," which is the better choice.)

4. It can indicate compound functions or job titles:

    In a cold real estate market, it is necessary that your realtor be an outstanding *promoter/marketer.*

    He had always admired Robert Redford, the *actor/director/conservationist.*

(Note that here the slash is shorthand for a list, separated by commas, which would serve equally well. This book frequently uses the slash to indicate two-word entry titles.)

5. When quoting more than one line of poetry within the text, the slash (followed by a space) indicates the end of each line:

> In "Commodities," the trader-turned-poet skewered his former profession:

> "Sugar was up while/ Coffee rose, only to subside/ Cattle sagged, hogs sagged/ Pork bellies fell to an all-time low/ And iced broilers were quiet."

The back slash has not evolved beyond its original use as a separator in computer disk directory sequences, as in C:\wine\france\red\cheap. But let us not pity a symbol whose singular use is measured in trillions each day.

SPELLING AND
COMMON CONFUSIONS

Spelling conventions are ruled by the status quo: if we all agreed to change the spelling of "physics" to "fizzicks," then we would take no notice of the word when we came across it on a page. But the more unfamiliar the misspelling, the more distracted from the message readers become.

You might have difficulty with the exact spelling of "euthanasia," but if you write it as "youth in asia," your readers will wonder why you have suddenly changed your topic. After a few of these stinkers, readers will simply stop reading what you have to say.

Software spell checkers will not help if you choose the wrong word. For example, if you use "principle" when you mean "principal," how is the spell check to know which one you meant? Words, such as the previous examples, that have the same sound but different meanings cause many of us no end of confusion. It's not that we don't know how to spell the words — we do — but either we know only one of the words, and use it incorrectly, or we know both words but can't keep their meanings straight. (See *Sound Alikes* for a list of such words.)

Any words that have similar meanings and spellings, like "founder" and "flounder," will consistently cause confusion, and then there are quite different words, like "infer" and "imply," whose meanings are often mistakenly reversed.

Finally, there are numerous single words whose correct usage puts most of us in a state of constant uncertainty. Examples are "enormity" and "fortuitous."

Good spellers always use a dictionary to verify spellings of words that give them trouble; this is what makes them good spellers. Poor spellers rarely check spellings and so their uncertainty is always with them.

On the Internet you can easily find lists of the most commonly misspelled words. Go through the list and figure out ways to remember the pesky ones. For example, the word "definite" contains the word "finite," which is spelled the way it is pronounced. "Accommodate" has two "c's" and two "m's." Figure out a way to remember that — Air Canada Centre two Mondays?

Here are the top five word-pair confusions. Chances are that you struggle with one or more of them. There are another 120 brain teasers in this section; when you master all of these, you will be uncommonly unconfused! And remember — if you have memorized the route you take to work, you can learn to improve your spelling.

1. It's/Its
2. You're/Your
3. Affect/Effect
4. Principal/Principle
5. Complimentary/Complementary

ACCEPT/EXCEPT

To *accept* means to receive or approve.

> He accepted the nomination as president of the West End Guinea Pig Association.

Except means "excluding."

> Everyone was there, except Reginald.

It also means "but."

> I'd do it, except I'm afraid.

ACCESSION/ASCENSION

Accession (ak-cession) means attaining a position of high rank, as in the Queen's accession to the throne, or Smith's accession to the presidency.

Ascension is the act of ascending (going up), the opposite of descending. Its use today is pretty much restricted to the Christian reference to Ascension Day, the ascent of Christ to Heaven on the fortieth day after Easter. As the above illustrates, *ascent* is the more widely used form.

ACETIC/ASCETIC/AESTHETIC

Acetic (pronounced a-see-tik): the acid, commonly known as vinegar.

Ascetic (pronounced as-se-tik): a person who lives what many would call a harsh life, since it is largely devoid of creature comforts. The word also describes such a person.

    "He's an ascetic."
    "He's ascetic in many ways."

Aesthetic (pronounced es-thet-ik): an appreciation of beauty, a sense of the beautiful; good taste. *Esthetic* is also an acceptable spelling.

AD/ADD

Ad is the accepted abbreviation for "advertisement" and, since *ad* is a complete word, a period at the end of it is unnecessary.

Add is the opposite of subtract.

A.D. (*anno domini*) refers to time after Christ, while B.C. refers to time *before* Christ, but the more neutral terms C.E. (Common Era) and B.C.E. (Before Common Era) are preferable.

"Wet weather really effect/affects Uncle Willy's arthritis."

Which one is correct?
(See *Affect/Effect* p. 139)

ADAPTATION/ADAPTION

There is no distinction in the meaning or use of these words. The verb form of both is "adapt," not to be confused with "adopt."

ADMITTANCE/ADMISSION

Admittance refers to physical entry — "No Admittance" — and *admission* means entry based upon the presentation of documentation or money, as in the admission price at a movie or the Admissions Department at a college.

In such cases one must go through admission before being admitted.

ADVERSE/AVERSE

Adverse means "harmful" or "against one's interest" and *averse* means "strongly disinclined."

> The shop was closed because of adverse weather.
> The medicine caused a strong adverse reaction.

> Bob and Betty are averse to having any pets in the house. (They have an *aversion* to pets.)

ADVISE/ADVICE

Also, devise/device, prophesy/prophecy. These are examples where the verb/noun pair differ in both spelling and pronunciation.

> ad-vize/ad-vice
> de-vize/de-vice
> praw-fe-sigh/praw-fe-see

License/licence and practise/practice follow the spelling but not the pronunciation change.

The British (and sensible) spelling distinction for such pairs is to spell the verb with "s" and the noun with "c." The Americans, however, use license and practice for both verb and noun, which leaves Canadians wondering whose lead they should follow (this time). But, as the British are consistent also with their spelling of the nouns "defence" and "offence" (the American is defense and offense), the best rule to follow is the British "s" (verb), "c" (noun) rule.

(See *Canadian/American/British Spelling*.)

Abuse (abuze) and abuse are representative of verb/noun pairs with "z" to "s" changes in pronunciation. Others are:

> close/close
> diffuse/diffuse
> disuse/disuse
> excuse/excuse
> house/house
> misuse/misuse
> refuse/refuse
> use/use

Examples:
> What's the use of having it, if you don't use it carefully?
> He refused to be thrown on the refuse heap of life.

AFFECT/EFFECT

> Inflation *affects* the economy. One of its *effects* is higher prices.

Whatever *affects* (changes) something has an *effect* (result). If you use *affect* as a verb and *effect* as a noun, you will have no trouble. Recalling that "cause and effect" means "cause and result" is a handy way of distinguishing between them.

Try to avoid using "impact" as a synonymous verb. Effects can be positive, negative or neutral. If you say, "How will the hiring decision impact the company?" it implies a concussive force that may not be an accurate description of the result.

Effect is also used as a verb, as in, "When will the change be effected?" but this use is no longer common, having been replaced by "go into effect."

ALIBI/EXCUSE

Alibi means "elsewhere." In the vocabulary of law, an alibi demonstrates that the accused was not at the scene of the crime when it was committed. Today, however, it has become pretty well synonymous with an *excuse* of any kind. As the name of a cocktail lounge, the "Alibi Room" incorporates both meanings quite nicely.

ALL RIGHT/ALRIGHT

All right in a phrase means "all correct" or, simply "Okay."

Alright is a variation that is not universally accepted, although some dictionaries are willing to recognize its existence. To be on the safe side, use "all right" all the time.

> "I have no respect for a person who can't spell a word more than one way."
> — MARK TWAIN (1845–1910)

ALL TOGETHER/ALTOGETHER

> They were standing all together in front of the church.
> Forty teams were represented altogether.

All together is used in the sense of everyone together in a unit. *Altogether* means "completely" or "totally."

ALLUDE/REFER

To *allude* is to make an indirect reference. To *refer* is to make a direct reference.

> "It's difficult to keep top talent in Canada," he said, alluding to Canadian-born entertainers who had moved to the United States. Later,

referring to this same problem, he mentioned Jim Carrey and Mike Myers of Toronto.

Elude, with which allude is often confused, means to avoid detection or to hide.

ALLUSION/ILLUSION/DELUSION

An *allusion* is a glancing reference, an *illusion* is a deceptive impression, and a *delusion is* a belief based on self-deception.

As he spoke about "the cowboy space age we live in," he made a number of allusions to *Star Wars.*

Although almost ruined, Felix kept his Mercedes, thus creating the illusion that he was a man to be reckoned with.

His psychiatrist accused him of having delusions of grandeur.

A LOT

This is **never** written as one word.

You've got a lot of nerve.
Thanks a lot, pal.

ALTERNATELY/ALTERNATIVELY

Alternatively refers to the existence of a different choice, an alternative.

Alternately means "by turns."

> They alternately drove and slept.
> "We could sit on our hands waiting for the
>   decision," he said, "or, alternatively, push
>   ahead and hope for the best."
> When the highway became hopelessly blocked,
>   they chose an alternative route.

(Today, many would say "alternate route," and this would be fine.)

ALTHOUGH/BUT

These words can't be used together in a sentence that has only two parts, because the *but* will cancel out the *although*. You can use one or the other, but not both:

> Although they tried to persuade me to return
> to Italy, but I knew that Canada was truly my
> home.

Revised:

> Although they tried to persuade me to return

to Italy, I knew that Canada was truly my home.

They tried to persuade me to return to Italy, but I knew that Canada was truly my home.

(See *Sentence Fragments* and *Run-on Sentences* for more examples.)

ANECDOTE/ANTIDOTE

An *anecdote* is a short reminiscence that illustrates some facet of a person's personality, often in an amusing way.

The young father related an anecdote about his three-year-old daughter, who suddenly exclaimed on a crowded bus: "But Dad! How does the baby get into the mummy's tummy?"

An *antidote* is any substance that neutralizes the effects of a poison. Thus, certain serums are the antidotes to (or for) certain snake poisons. By extension, antidote can be used to mean the cure for anything unpleasant.

His jokes were a welcome antidote to the pain she felt.

ANYWAY/ANYWAYS
Anyways — for the moment, *anyway* — is as bad as ain't, which makes it unacceptable except in jest or quotation.

APOPLECTIC/EPILEPTIC
Figuratively, as an exaggeration of the effect of a sudden shock on someone, one can say, "I was apoplectic . . . he looked apoplectic . . . everyone went apoplectic," but never "epileptic," which describes the loss of muscular control.

Incidentally, the two words constitute a minor tongue-twister.

ARCTIC/ANTARCTIC
Each word has two "c's."

ASSURE/ENSURE/INSURE
They all mean "to make certain," but are used in slightly different ways:

> I assure you that I will attend.
> You have my assurance that I will not fail you.

I ensure (but not ensure *you*) that I will attend.

Can we ensure compliance with all the policies?

Some would use *insure* interchangeably with the two last examples, but *insure* is generally reserved for reference to financial guarantees (as in *insurance*).

ASTRONOMER/ASTROLOGER

Perhaps, because of the increased popularity of astrology, the distinction between these words has become milky.

An *astronomer* is a scientist who studies the planets and the stars without regard to any psychic or physical influence they might exert upon human beings.

An *astrologer* is concerned with the changing relationships of the heavenly bodies as they are believed to be predictors of the course of human conduct.

BAZAAR/BIZARRE

Bazaar is an Arab word for "market." In North America it usually refers to a general sale of second-hand items for charitable purposes, as in a church bazaar.

Bizarre means out of the ordinary, as in bizarre dress or bizarre behaviour.

BEAR/BARE

As a noun, *bear* describes an animal; as a verb, it means to carry and, by extension, to endure, withstand, or put up with.

> Those columns will not bear the weight of the roof.
> They arrived bearing gifts for all.

> Please bear with me. I'll try to finish as soon as possible.
> I can't bear it when you behave like that.

The past tense is *bore*.

Bare means stripped to the essentials, empty, naked, as in "the cupboard was bare."

BIAS/BIASED

Bias is the noun, *biased* is the adjective or verb form:

> They refer to a distortion of judgment, a preference or a prejudice.

> His opinion is obviously biased, since he stands to lose money if the deal goes ahead.

> His bias in favour of investing profit did not sit well with his partners.

Spelling Quiz
Only three words in English end with "-ceed."
Only one word ends with "-sede."
What are they?
(See *Ceed/Sede/Cede* p. 151)

BIWEEKLY

If you mean **once every two**, use "biweekly,"
"bimonthly," "biennially" or "biyearly."

> The magazine is published every two weeks,
> or biweekly.

If you mean **twice every time unit**, use semiweekly,
semimonthly, or biannually.

Obviously, this is very confusing for everyone.
Plant lovers know that "annual" means once a year
and "biannual" means twice a year. Beyond that, it's
easy to make your meaning clear by avoiding such
words altogether. Substitute with expressions such
as "every month," "quarterly," or "six times a year."

BURNT/LEARNT

These forms used to be confined to British English, with *learnt* being the most persistent example. But the distinction is not so rigid anymore: the toast could be "burned" or *burnt*; the dream "dreamed" or "dreamt"; the juice "spilled" or "spilt."

"Spoilt," and "spelt," however, like *learnt*, sound quaint to North American ears, which are so very finely tuned to linguistic conformity.

CALLUS/CALLOUS

Callus is the name for the toughened areas of skin, particularly on the hands, that are caused by sustained manual work. The plural is calluses.

Callous describes an insensitive and rough personality or deed.

CANADIAN/AMERICAN/BRITISH SPELLING

It has been said that a developing Canada simultaneously reported to two head offices, one British the other American, and this dual influence is still visible in our spelling conventions. As every-one knows, we write "colour" and "centre," while the Americans write "color" and "center." The American preference for dispensing with superfluous letters extends to dropping the double "l" in "traveller" and the "e" in "judgement." These changes are bound to creep into Canadian usage. Who cares anymore whether we use "gray" or "grey"? And the spelling of "maneuver" is easier to remember than the British form, "manoeuvre." The important thing is to remain consistent and avoid such obvious mixing as "the rumor put me in good humour." A good dictionary will provide and identify both spellings.

A final point: words such as "authorize" may be spelled with either "s" or "z." In North American usage, "ize" is the preferred form, but many common words still retain "ise." (See *Advise/advice* for a similar spelling difficulty.)

analyze	advertise
apologize	compromise
authorize	exercise
criticize	merchandise
paralyze	supervise
realize	
summarize	

CAREER/CAREEN

The car careened down the road.

To *career* means to move rapidly. To *careen* means to lurch, or swerve from side to side.

Their similar appearance and the compatibility of their meanings, as in the example above, have all but eliminated *career* from popular usage.

Incidentally, the noun *career* means a rapid pursuit, although this has been forgotten for so long that we now speak of "pursuing a career."

CAVALRY/CALVARY
Confusion could result in some embarrassment. The first term describes soldiers on horseback, while the second (always capitalized) is the name of the place where Christ was executed.

CEED/SEDE/CEDE
Only three words in English contain -*ceed*: exceed, proceed, succeed.

Only one word contains -*sede*: supersede.

All others with this sound are spelled -*cede*: precede, recede, concede, secede, for example.

CENSOR/CENSURE
To *censor* means to examine, judge, or be responsible for prohibiting in public what is considered to be objectionable.

To *censure* means to blame or criticize.

> Richard Nixon censored the transcripts of his
> White House tapes and was censured for
> doing so.

Censor is not a synonym of "prevent," and you cannot censor someone from doing something. You can only censor the behaviour and then *censure* the person for having done it.

> "*Complementary Breakfast*," reads a notice in
> your hotel room.
>
> Does that mean it's free?
> (See *Complement/Compliment* p. 155)

CHANGEABLE/SOLVABLE

When "able" is added to certain words, the preceding "e" is sometimes dropped and sometimes retained. The following is a list of the most persistently confusing words in this category:

advisable	moveable or movable
changeable	provable
driveable	saleable or salable

knowledgeable   serviceable

likeable or   solvable
   likable   traceable

manageable   unforgivable

mileage or   usable
   milage

CHAUVINIST/SEXIST

Chauvinism means fanatical devotion to one's country, and, by extension, a narrow-minded and superior devotion to one's group. *Chauvinist* is now used almost exclusively to mean male chauvinist, which is a pity, since all sorts of people are chauvinists of one kind or another.

A *sexist* discriminates against the opposite sex.

CHILDISH/CHILDLIKE

Childish is a scornful term and is almost synonymous with silly and immature.

When applied to adults, *childlike* describes a person who has managed to retain a certain innocence and freshness towards life.

Similarly applied, "juvenile" is a derogatory term, while "boyish" and "girlish" are usually favourable terms when applied to adults.

CHOOSE/CHOSE

Choose (chuze) is the present tense of the verb; *chose* (choze) is the past tense. The noun is "choice."

> He chose not to choose, and that was his choice.

CLIMACTIC/CLIMATIC

Climactic is the adjective form of "climax," and *climatic* is the adjective form of "climate." If indeed a new ice age is dawning, we could yet experience "climactic climatic conditions."

"Acclimatize" means to grow accustomed to a particular environment. There is no such word as "climatize."

COMPARE TO/WITH

When you compare one thing *to* another, you are suggesting a similarity between them.

> He compared rock music to the sound of small animals in pain.

> Roderick's logic seems to consist of comparing some sort of apple to some sort of orange.

It might help to remember that "compare to" means "liken."

When you compare one thing *with* another, you are making a detailed comparison.

> It is depressing to compare today's prices with those of 1988.
>
> (It is impossible to compare today's prices *to* those of 1988 because they are so different.)
>
> When he compared the appeal of the Beatles with the appeal of the Rolling Stones, he found that more people preferred to listen to the Beatles.
>
> Compared with other Pacific coast cities, Vancouver is still unspoiled.

COMPLEMENT/COMPLIMENT

To *complement* means to complete the whole, as in the ship's complement (its entire crew). Or, her sweater complements her skirt (completes the outfit).

> Soft lighting complemented the plush leather sofas.

To *compliment* means to give or receive praise or congratulations.

They complimented him for having quit smoking.

For the adjective forms, a person who is ready with praise is said to be *complimentary* and, by extension, a *complimentary* breakfast is offered as a compliment to the guest, at no charge.

COMPRISE/CONSTITUTE/COMPOSE

Never in the history of language have so many people had so much trouble with so few words.

To *comprise* means to include, to embrace, to consist of.

To *constitute* and to *compose* are synonyms, meaning to make up, or to form. *Compose* is better used in the passive voice ("is composed of") and *constitute* in the active voice ("constitutes the").

The whole comprises the parts.
The parts constitute the whole.
The whole is composed of its parts.

Or:

Something comprises the elements of which it is composed.

It takes some hard thinking to get these straight. Here is an example of the use of each.

Middle English comprises the various dialects
of Late Old English.

Buses, subways, and streetcars constitute the
transit system.

The transit system is composed of buses, etc.

The band was composed of a lead singer, two
guitars, keyboard, and drums.

A lead singer, two guitars, etc. constitute the
band.

Enron Executives Receive Just Deserts.
Baseball Bully's Just Dessert.

These newspaper headlines are each intending
to convey the sense of "just reward." Which one
is correct?

(See *Dessert/Desert* p. 162)

COMPULSIVE/IMPULSIVE

To be *compulsive* is to exhibit obsessive behaviour
and to be *impulsive* is to exhibit spontaneous
behaviour. Both are considered to be problematic
traits.

Thus, people are described as being compulsive
talkers, eaters, drinkers, gamblers, shoppers.

Impulsive behaviour is acting on impulse,
without sufficient forethought:

In a hot real-estate market, many couples
make impulsive offers just to stay in the game.

CONDONE

To *condone* means to approve by disregard and
without protest. You don't have to agree with what
you condone.

He was irked by their long lunches, but he
condoned them rather than speak up.

To *condone* does not mean to disapprove of or to
condemn, although it is sometimes mistakenly used
this way.

CONFIDANT/CONFIDENT

You share your secrets with a *confidant* and don't
pronounce the "t" (in the French manner), although
you may not be terribly *confident* (assured) that the
secrets will remain secret for long.

CONSEQUENTLY/SUBSEQUENTLY

Consequently means "as a result," and *subsequently*
means "after" or "following."

There was a mechanical problem with their plane, and consequently they were delayed. Subsequently, they were informed that the airline had rebooked them in First Class.

CONTEMPTIBLE/CONTEMPTUOUS

Contempt means "scorn" or "disrespect."

If you think someone or something is deserving of contempt, then you think it is *contemptible*.

If you are feeling contempt for someone or something, then you are *contemptuous* of them.

> She thought his behaviour toward her was contemptible.
>
> He was contemptuous of her new way of life.

CONTINUOUS/CONTINUED

Continuous means without cease for a period of time, as in "continuous music from noon until midnight."

Continued refers to a sequence that is broken and then resumed after an interval, as in "continued on page 78," or "to be continued next week."

The adverbs are "continuously" and "continually."

COPYRIGHT/COPYWRITER

A *copyright* is the assertion of the legal right to a particular written (or other) work. The past tense of the verb is "copyrighted," and is usually employed as an adjective: "this material is copyrighted; this is copyrighted material."

A *copywriter* writes advertising copy.

A playwright writes plays.

CORPS/CORPSE

A *corps* (capitalized when it applies to the military) is a body or organization of men and women with specific duties. The word is pronounced as "core."

A *corpse* is a dead human, and thus it is unnecessary to say "dead corpse." The body of a dead animal is a "carcass."

In the midst of a party honouring the Irish playwright George Bernard Shaw, the excited hostess rushed up to him and asked, "Are you enjoying yourself, Mr. Shaw?"

Shaw carefully surveyed the room. "Yes, Madam, indeed I am," he replied. "But that is all I am enjoying."
Is this the remark of an egoist or egotist?
(See *Egoist/Egotist* p. 165)

DECENT/DESCENT

For *decent*, the emphasis is on "de" while for *descent*, the accent is on "scent." *Decent* means morally acceptable, or presentable (the opposite of "indecent"), and *descent* means "lowering" or "falling," the opposite of "ascent."

DEFINITE/DEFINITIVE

Definite means "certain," whereas *definitive* signals a reference or defining point by which all others of that classification are measured.

> I will give you a definite (as opposed to a tentative) answer tomorrow.

> Each successive biography of famous artists claims to be the definitive work.

DENOTE/CONNOTE

Denote is literal meaning, while *connote* (*connotation* is its most common form) is figurative meaning.

> The parents told their young daughter Camilla that Florence was running for the office of trustee, but Camilla feared she didn't have a chance, because it was obvious that she wasn't a fast runner.

DESERT/DESSERT

Dessert refers to the last course of a meal and that is its only meaning.

Desert has several meanings and pronunciations.

As a noun, it has two meanings. The most common is an arid, usually sandy, landscape, as in "Sahara Desert." The first syllable of the word ("de-") is stressed.

The newspaper headline on p. 157 features the second meaning, which comes from the French word for "deserving." Since its pronunciation is identical to *dessert*, and *dessert* is seen as a sort of final reward, it is tempting to imagine that "just deserts" is the correct phrase. Alas, it is not.

Desert is also used as a verb, meaning to abandon, but with this usage the second, rather than the first, syllable is stressed.

DIFFERENT FROM/THAN

Save *different than* for the awkward constructions which would necessitate "*different from* that which. . . ." *Than* is used only when it is followed by a subject and a verb.

Thus:

His book is different from mine.
Each day is different from the rest.

This tobacco is very different than it used to be.
She looks much different than she did
   yesterday.

DISCOVER/INVENT

You *discover* something that is already there. You *invent* something new.

Of course, nothing prevents a manufacturer from inventing a product, and then claiming to have discovered it.

DISCRIMINATING/DISCRIMINATORY

A *discriminating* individual is able to make subtle distinctions between or among apparent similarities. This ability is frequently assumed to be a sign of refined taste.

Howard's vast knowledge of Australian wines
had given him a very discriminating palate.

A *discriminatory* individual, on the other hand, is an individual who discriminates by separating or rejecting on the basis of perceived differences. Such an individual is guilty of bias or prejudice.

The supervisor was charged with several
discriminatory acts directed at female
employees.

DISINTERESTED/UNINTERESTED

The first term means unbiased, impartial, of no opinion. The second term means a lack of interest, and its meaning would appear to be obvious.

However, *disinterested* is so frequently used when *uninterested* is meant that it suggests many people are loath to say they are not interested. Thus, *disinterested* is mistakenly used as a euphemism for *uninterested*.

DISSOCIATE/DISASSOCIATE

Disassociate came first, but the meanings of these words are identical and their usages are interchangeable.

When you no longer want to associate with a group, you *dissociate* or *disassociate* yourself from it. In psychology, dissociate refers to a person who is out of touch with what is occurring in the moment.

DISTRUST/MISTRUST

Practically speaking, *distrust* is a synonym for "I don't trust," while *mistrust* carries the connotation of wariness — "I don't fully trust." This implied difference is so slight, however, that the words are generally accepted to be synonymous.

DIVED/DOVE

As the past tense form of the verb "dive," either form is acceptable, but the correct past participle form is "dived" only:

> They *dived* (or *dove*) to 150 metres; they hadn't dived that deep before.

EGOISM/EGOTISM

We all have a certain (or "healthy") amount of *egoism*, a realization of the relative importance of self. To qualify as an *egoist*, however, you need a pretty good dose of it — sufficient, at least, to make you a leader rather than a follower.

Egotists, on the other hand, are consumed with themselves. They're boastful, conceited and arrogant. They'll tell you they're great even when they're not. (But, alas, sometimes they are.)

ELICIT/ILLICIT

Elicit is a verb meaning to draw out or to provoke, as in: "The politician's outrageous statements elicited a gasp from the crowd."

> Management attempted to elicit agreement from their staff to work overtime without extra pay.

Illicit is an adjective meaning illegal or unlawful, as in illicit drugs.

EMPATHIZE/SYMPATHIZE

Confusion about the meaning of these two terms is not surprising, as both are related to the expression of feelings of compassion.

The key to understanding the difference is in the nature of the compassion.

Sympathy is more detached than *empathy*; it denotes a feeling *for*, rather than a feeling *with*. We feel sympathy towards the unfortunate plights of others, and we may signal this by an expression of pity or by sending a sympathy card.

When we *empathize*, we identify with the feelings of another person; we participate emotionally with their situation. A crying child may trigger other children to cry, an empathetic (or empathic) response at its most elemental.

ENORMOUS/ENORMITY

Enormity is generally used as if it were the noun form of *enormous*. It is not. It means "monstrous wickedness," and, though it relates to moral degree, it has nothing to do with physical degree.

The confusion is compounded by such phrases as "the enormity of the Nazi crimes," in which we cannot help equating the *enormity* with the *enormous* number of people involved.

ENVISAGE/ENVISION
The difference between these words is slight but worthwhile.

To *envisage* means an attempt to imagine something (often a state of affairs) as a future reality.

To *envision* means to conceptualize or foresee.

> He tried to envisage a peaceful world, yet he couldn't envision anything changing.

ETC.
Never "ect." and usually preceded by a comma. (See *Latin Abbreviations*.)

FARTHER/FURTHER
Use *farther* when you refer to physical distance.

> Montreal is *farther* from Toronto than Ottawa.

Use *further* to express figurative distance.

> He took the argument one step *further*.

In speech you can get away with using either; but in writing, be aware of the difference.

FATAL/FATEFUL

> "I'll never forget that fatal day."

Fatal, of course, means "deadly," and it's difficult to imagine a day being fatal. However, a *fateful* day, meaning a day that affected one's destiny, might easily have had fatal consequences.

> "I'll never forget the fateful day of the accident that killed my cat Smudge."
> He brought the fateful news that he was being transferred to Spot, Nebraska.

FIX/REPAIR

To *fix* can mean to *repair*, but it also means "to secure, or fasten," though that meaning has been largely replaced by "affixed" or "attached."

When *repair* is meant, we tend to use *fix* for relatively small or familiar objects (fix the car, the door hinge, the lawnmower), but *repair* when the object is large, unfamiliar or mechanically complicated:

> The repair of the aircraft wing took several weeks.

FLAGGING/LAGGING

One has *flagging* spirits, not *lagging* spirits. *Flagging* means to become dispirited or to lose interest, and *lagging* means to fall back or lose pace.

> After eight hours of playing bridge, his concentration began to flag.

> During the march, the sick and disabled lagged far behind.

FLAMMABLE/INFLAMMABLE

Inflammable came first (from inflame), but when its use as a warning became widespread it was thought by many (not without reason) to mean "not flammable." So *inflammable* became *flammable*, which seems to convey the intended message. Even today, however, its use is not universal, and you should be cautious also with liquids marked *inflammable*.

FLAUNT/FLOUT

If you jaywalk ten feet away from a police officer, you are *flouting* the law; that is, treating it with disregard and contempt.

To *flaunt* means to make an ostentatious show of, and thus one could say that, while dictators flaunt their authority, they also flout international law.

FOREWORD/FORWARD

Foreword means "first word," literally, "word before." It describes a brief introduction to a book by someone aquainted with the author's life and work; if written by the author, it is generally called a *preface*.

Forward, of course, means "ahead," as in "putting your best foot forward.

When the sense is "before," as in "foreword" or "forearm," the word you want is *fore*, not "for." A list of *fore* words follows.

fore-and-aft	foremost
forebode	forerunner
forecast	foresee
foreclose	foreshadow
forefather	foresight
foregone	foreskin
foreground	forestall
foreknowledge	foretell
foreman	forethought

FORMER/LATTER

When referring to two people or things already stated, the first mentioned is indicated by *former*, and *latter* is used to refer to the second thing mentioned.

> When George and Pete struck pay dirt, the former high-tailed it south, while the latter laid his gold dust on the bar.

The Globe and Mail, July 23, 2005
"Most [Chinese currency] notes bare a portrait of the late Chairman Mao Zedong."

Can you bear it?

FORTUITOUS/GRATUITOUS

Fortuitous (for-too-i-tus) simply means "by chance," (as in "it just happened that . . .") not necessarily by lucky chance, and "fortuitously" is certainly not a synonym for "luckily." It must be admitted, however, that one is not likely to use the word to describe an unhappy random occurrence.

> Fortuitously, I ran into an old colleague at the conference, and we decided to spend the afternoons playing golf.

Fortuitous does not mean "free, without charge." That word is *gratuitous*, whose root meaning is "voluntary." Thus, a "gratuity" is a favour in return for a service. Gratuitous has come to mean "unnecessary" or "unwarranted," as in "gratuitous criticism" or "gratuitous sex/violence in today's movies."

FOUNDER/FLOUNDER

As a verb, to *founder* can be used to mean "disabled" or, with a horse, to become "suddenly lame," as in "The lead horse foundered on the last turn."

However, its most widespread use is in the sense of "sinking beneath the water," as in "The ship foundered off the coast of Newfoundland." In this sense it can mean either that the ship's deck is awash and it lies disabled, or that it has sunk to the bottom.

Flounder means to move clumsily and with great difficulty. In a metaphoric sense, one can, and many do, flounder through life.

FULSOME

Believe it or not, this word means "disgustingly excessive," a meaning that cannot possibly be construed as being complimentary. All those comments that you've heard about "*fulsome* dinners, evenings, bodies, etc." are quite the opposite of what you (and likely the speaker as well) had imagined them to mean.

For a full hour, the sportswriters directed their fulsome envy toward the young golf champion.

GAMUT/GANTLET/GAUNTLET

Gamut means the complete range (from A to Z), and these days has been largely replaced by such phrases as "they have everything."

In the old days — the very old days — men threw down the *gauntlet* (the glove), symbolically offering a challenge. According to the Jesuits, the Iroquois forced victims to "run the *gantlet*," a corridor of warriors armed with clubs.

In fact, both *gauntlet* and *gantlet* are acceptable today in the expression "run the gantlet," meaning to undergo a severe trial.

GOT/GOTTEN

The concern here is whether the past participle of "have got" as in "I've never got over it," is *got* or *gotten*. The only thing that can be said in favour of either is that because *got* is also the form of the present tense — "He's got a car" — some ambiguity is possible. Does this mean that he has a car, or that he's recently bought a car? Similarly, if you say, "He's just got a Honda," some ambiguity is possible. Does this mean that he can't afford a better car, or that he's recently gotten a Honda? *Gotten* is the most common form in North American usage, but either will do.

HANGED/HUNG

Paintings (and Christmas stockings) are *hung*; people are *hanged*.

However, "they hung him" has the sound of barbarity and, on such occasions, niceties of language are probably irrelevant.

HARK/HARP ON

To *hark* means to listen closely, as in "Hark, the herald angels sing." Its use is archaic.

To *hark back*, however, means to return to some point in the past — loosely, "to recall" — as in "The wools and cottons of today's fashions hark back to a more primitive time."

To *harp on* means to dwell vocally on something so much as to annoy.

John lost $20 yesterday and has been harping on it ever since.

HISTORIC/HISTORICAL

Historic refers to the event, or the occasion — an historic moment.

Historical means, "relating significantly to history."

> For the moment, at least, suburbia is not historical in any way.

(Not be confused with "hysterical.")

HYPHENATED WORDS

When two or more words are combined to produce one meaning, the resulting compound might be written as separate words (e.g. trade name), it might be joined by one or more hyphens (father-in-law), or it might be written as a single word (timetable). When written as separate words, the compound is known as "open"; when written as a single word, it is considered "closed."

The form of compound nouns, such as in the examples above, may evolve from open, to hyphenated, to closed. Such an evolution turned "bookkeeper" into the rather odd-looking word it is today. Most compound nouns, however, display a permanent form, and this is the spelling that will be found in an up-to-date dictionary.

Guidelines for the use of hyphens with prefixes

and suffixes are not consistent, but the trend is to avoid them unless the resulting compound produces a confusing pattern of letters. Frequency of use reduces the initial confusion. Thus, where "co-operate" was always hyphenated to eliminate "coop," it no longer causes confusion today. Some style manuals include "reedit" in this modernization, but traditionalists will insist on "re-edit" to ensure instant clarity, in addition to combinations such as "deescalate," "deemphasize," and "semiannual."

There is general agreement that hyphens are always used with the prefixes "self," "quasi" and "ex," as in "self-paced," "quasi-liberated," and "ex-husband."

Here are some additional guidelines:

1. Compound adjectives are hyphenated before the noun but are generally open when used after the noun:

> They chose a sea-green colour for the
> living room walls.
> The living walls are sea green.

> Her aunt was a well-known actor.
> Her aunt was well known.

2.   This also applies to prepositional phrases:

> The minister gave an off-the-record
> interview to the press.
> The interview was off the record.

> An up-to-date chronology of events was
> provided.
> The chronology was up to date.

3.   Hyphenate fractions and also numbers from twenty-one to ninety-nine (see *Numbers*):

> One-quarter, three-eighths

4.   Never use a hyphen with combined directions:

> southeast, northwest

5.   A series of compounds requires a suspension of the fully-hyphenated form:

> The bank has eliminated its two-, three-,
> and four-year mortgages.
> It now offers only short- and long-term
> mortgages.
> (Note that a space is provided after the
> suspended hyphen when no comma
> follows.)

6. In addition to "bookkeeper," the compounds "roommate" and "granddaughter" also retain their collided consonants.

IE/EI

"I" before "e" except after "c" is a useful spelling rule. Here are the most common *ie/ei* words you're ever likely to use.

1. "i" before "e": believe, retrieve, achieve, chief, siege, field.

2. Except after "c": receive, deceive, conceit, ceiling, perceive, conceive.

3. Words like "neighbour" ("ei" pronounced "ay"): weigh, sleigh, deign, feign, rein, Seine, vein, beige, eight, freight, inveigh, inveigle, reign, veil, heinous, sheikh.

4. Others: neither, seize, weird, leisure, forfeit, surfeit, counterfeit, height, eiderdown, heifer, foreign.

IMMIGRATE/EMIGRATE

You *emigrate* from a country and *immigrate* to a country. All immigrants, therefore, emigrated from their homelands.

IN CAMERA

When a meeting or discussion is held *in camera*, it means behind closed doors, in private, without press or photographers.

It does not, of course, mean that the proceedings are filmed.

INCIDENCE/INCIDENT/INSTANCE

Incidence refers to rate of occurrence, *incident* refers to one occurrence, and *instance* refers to one example.

> The incidence of typhoid is lowest in naturally cold environments.
>
> In one celebrated incident he tried to do a headstand on the bar.
>
> That was just one instance, of course, where he'd had too much to drink.

Remember, also, "for instance," meaning "for example."

IN CONTRAST/ON THE CONTRARY

These two phrases are not interchangeable, although they often appear together in the same list of transitional phrases.

Try using them the same way:

> He's not rich; on the contrary, he is very poor.
> He's not rich; in contrast, he's very poor.

The first is correct, but the second is not. Why?

Because *in contrast* doesn't work when the subject is the same in both clauses. To use it correctly, you would have to say

> He is rich. In contrast, she is poor.

In summary:

Use *in contrast* when the subjects of the clauses are different and use *on the contrary* when the subjects are the same.

INCREDIBLE/INCREDULOUS

Incredible means "unbelievable," and *incredulous* means "disbelieving."

> His mental capacity was incredible.
> It left me incredulous.

The positive forms of these are words are credible, meaning "believable," and credulous, meaning "gullible" (willing to believe).

INFER/IMPLY

When you *infer*, you reach a conclusion (not necessarily correct) based on the evidence at hand.

> We can *infer* from the sad state of his teeth that he hasn't been to a dentist for some time.

To *imply* means "to suggest or hint subtly."

> "Sharon," John began, quickly pulling in his gut. "What are you *implying*?"
> "I'm not *implying* anything."
> "Then why do you keep mentioning the exercise program at the Y?"

In a prominent newspaper, a publisher advertises the success of a bestselling novel:

Now In It's Fifth Printing!

Do you have an exclamation of your own for this publisher?

IT'S/ITS

Look at it this way:

1.	2.	3.	4.
I	I'm	my	mine
you	you're	your	yours
he	he's	his	his
she	she's	her	hers
it	*it's*	*its*	*its*
we	we're	our	ours
you	you're	your	yours
they	they're	their	theirs

Column one lists the personal pronouns. Column two contains contractions of the verb "to be." (He's, she's, and it's are also contractions of the verb "to have" — "It's been a nice day.")

Columns three and four list the possessive forms. Notice that, as with his and hers, "its" has no apostrophe.

If you still have difficulty keeping this straight, check what you mean to say each time you use "it's" or "its." Do you mean possession or are you simply using the contraction of "it is" or "it has?"

It's great. (It is great.)
It's been great. (It has been great.)
The car lost its wheels. (It is wheels?)

JIBE/JIVE

When two things match or agree, they *jibe* — an opposite would be "clash."

> The accused gave their stories separately, and they didn't jibe.

Jive was once a colloquialism meaning "nonsense." (At one time "guff" was a synonym; "jive" is also outdated; "crap" is probably the most polite version in use today. How times change.)

> Don't give me that jive, man.

LEACH/LEECH

If you are an engineer or geologist, you'd better get these straight before you begin writing your first report on soils and substrata.

A *leech* is the blood-sucking worm once used to draw poison from a wound, and now the chief horror of summer cottage swimmers.

Leach is the word the soil engineer uses to describe the process by which a liquid, usually water, penetrates a material (like your basement walls).

LEAD/LED

> "Lead me to your leader," said the blind
> Martian.
> They led him to their leader.
> So far, Hornsby has led a rather unsavory life.

The past tense of *lead* is *led*. The metal, lead, is pronounced the same way.

LEND/BORROW

Lend money *to* someone, *borrow* money *from* someone.

> He wouldn't lend me any money, so I
> borrowed ten from Ralph.

When you borrow, you have made a loan. Although one hears "loan me" for "lend me," the latter is the preferred form.

LIABLE/APT/LIKELY

You would likely say "the baby is liable to fall," but "the cat is apt to jump"; you might say "he's apt to forget" with a smile, but "he's liable to forget" with a frown.

The meanings of *apt* and *liable* are extremely close but generally differ in that *liable* carries an implied warning, the hint of an impending negative, whereas *apt* simply means that the action would suit the person or the circumstance.

Likely, or "very likely," indicates a high probability.

LIBEL/SLANDER

Both words mean "to defame maliciously," *libel* in print or picture, *slander* in speech. Thus, the phrase "verbal slander" is redundant. If you're about to do either, consider first that libel is much easier to prove.

LIE/LAY/LIE

These verbs have the following principal parts:

Lie — to recline: lie, lay, lain, lying.
Lay — to place: lay, laid, laid, laying.
Lie — to tell a falsehood: lie, lied, lied, lying.

Except for its similar spelling, there is no problem with the use of *lie* (to tell a falsehood). The confusion is with *lie* (to recline) and *lay* (to place).

Lie is never followed by an object:
> Let's lie down on this moss.
> I lay awake all night.
> John is upstairs, lying down.

Lay is always followed by an object:
> They are laying the carpet today.
> Mabel, the hen, laid two eggs this morning.
> Lay our precious Ming Dynasty vase over
> there, if you please.

The confusion arises partly because the past tense of *lie* is identical with the infinitive form of *lay* (I lay down, lay it there) and partly because in popular usage, *lay* is used to mean *lie*:

> Lay yourself down.
> I was just layin' around.

No doubt American popular music has had something to do with this. At any rate, the difference between *lie* and *lay* is clear and should be followed in writing.

LOATH/LOATHE

> I am *loath* (reluctant) to lend my weirdo son
> the car.

I *loathe* (strongly dislike) eggplant.

The first (an adjective) has the same sound as "oath"; the second (a verb) rhymes with "clothe."

LOOSE/LOSE

Lose (looze) — *lose* a game, a friend, a pair of glasses.

Loose is never pronounced with the "z" sound. It means "free from constraint" — "he has a loose tooth."

Loosen, a verb, means to "make loose."

The forms of these verbs are:

> lose: lost, lost, losing.
> loosen: loosened, loosened, loosening.

MAJORITY/PLURALITY

A *majority* means more than 50% and should be used only opposite a stated or implied minority — if you mean simply "most," as in, "The majority of the cars were Cadillacs," then say "most."

In an election where there are only two candidates, one of them always wins by a *majority*; in an election of three or more candidates, the one receiving the greatest number of votes has a *plurality* — usually expressed as a percentage — and, if lucky enough to gain more than a 50% plurality, wins a majority of the votes as well.

MARTIAL/MARITAL

Martial pertains to the military — *martial* law, *martial* music.

Marital pertains to marriage.

> When a government is overthrown, there is martial law.

> When a married couple is having problems with their relationship, they are having marital difficulties.

MISSPELL/MISSPEAK

Yes, they do have a double "s" and so do "misspend," "misstep," "misstate," and "Mississippi."

You could remember them as All-America Spelling Queens: Miss Pell, Miss Peak, Miss Pend, Miss Tep, Miss Tate, and Miss Issippi.

MOMENTARILY/PRESENTLY/CURRENTLY

These words are misused all the time, especially by radio personalities: "We will have weather and sports momentarily."

Momentarily means "for a moment," not, as implied by the radio host, "within the next minute or two." Here is an example of proper usage:

> While stretching to hammer in another pylon, the rock climber momentarily lost his grip, and almost fell a thousand feet.

Presently means "soon"; it does not mean "at the moment" or "now." Thus, presently should have been the choice of the radio host.

Currently means "at the moment," or "at present," as in, "Currently she's studying in Russia."

The current issue of a magazine is the most recent issue.

MOOT

A *moot* question or point (the words it most often precedes) is a debatable one, because it is unresolved.

However, today it is more frequently used to imply a dead or irrelevant issue:

Whether or not he was guilty of the crime is a moot question, since he cannot be retried.

Opposition to the appointment of the new CEO became moot when it was disclosed that the company had filed for bankruptcy protection.

NAUSEOUS/NAUSEATED

One feels *nauseated* by a *nauseous* (naw-zee-us, or, naw-shus) smell.

Nauseous means "causing nausea"; *nauseated* means "experiencing nausea."

Rotten eggs give off a nauseous (or nauseating) smell.

The poor quality food made him feel nauseated.

NICKEL

The word describes the metal as well as the American and Canadian five-cent piece. It is never spelled "nickle."

NOUNS ENDING IN "OR"

If you have trouble with these words, you should list them as you come across them — sometimes they're hard to remember.

advisor	instructor
or adviser	investor
contractor	predictor
councillor	supervisor
counsellor	surveyor
dictator	survivor
director	victor
doctor	

Three commonly used words that end in "-er" are controller, forecaster, and observer.

OBTUSE/ABSTRUSE

An *obtuse* person is slow-witted and literally, "not very sharp" (as in an obtuse angle). In conversation, it is sometimes used as a label for someone who is being deliberately uncooperative ("Don't be so obtuse!"). It does not mean "stubborn," although it is often used as such.

Abstruse people are difficult to understand, perhaps because they talk over everyone's head, or simply because they don't make any sense. Abstruse is often used to refer to theories that can be understood by only a few people.

> When you were in school, was it the principal who made the morning announcements, or the principle?
>
> (see *Principal/Principle* p. 199)

ONCE IN A WHILE

Not "once *and* a while," which doesn't make sense. The mistake is probably caused by our lazy pronunciation of "and" in "once and for all" ("once 'n"), which makes it sound the same as "once in."

ORIENT/ORIENTATE

Both words mean to "set in the right direction" and "get your bearings," as in "*orient* yourself to your surroundings."

The noun for both is "orientation."

When used to mean "directed or concerned with," as in "results-oriented," or "client-oriented," *orientated* is never used.

PARAMETER

Since this word is almost invariably used as a synonym for "perimeter" or "limit," it is perhaps futile to point out that this is not what it means. However, for what it's worth, *parameter* refers to a restricting constant or variable, as in, "Terrorism will be a parameter of the 2000s."

PARANOID

Paranoid is not a synonym for "scared" or "afraid." You are not *paranoid* of snakes, you are scared of them.

Paranoia is an unreasonable fear of persecution. A person suffering from paranoia is a paranoiac, or a *paranoid* individual.

PARISH/PERISH

No wonder spelling in English is so difficult!

Parish refers to the members of a church; *perish* is a verb meaning "expire" or "die."

The "publish or perish" imperative is the engine of academic scholarship.

In another variation, we often see the phrase "non-perishable foods only" at food bank drop-offs.

PASSED/PAST

The past tense of pass is *passed.*

> We passed a Corvette driven by a clown.
> Wendell passed out when he heard the news.
> The storm passed quickly.

Past has a number of meanings:

> We went past a Cadillac.
> The Wild West is a thing of the past.
> Get off two stops past (beyond) Main Street.

PEDAL/PEDDLE

You *pedal* a bicycle to work.

If you *peddle* wares door-to-door, you are a peddlar: in British spelling, a pedlar.

(In North America, the latter meanings are essentially obsolete today, this selling method having been replaced by online shopping.)

PERCENT/PERCENTAGE/PROPORTION

Percentage is the rate of *percent,* as in "A large percentage of the goods shipped by air are lost to organized crime." Percentage is frequently used when "number" would suffice: "A large percentage of cigar smokers are divorced or single."

And it is worth remembering that when you say "large number," you usually mean "most," and when you say "small number," you usually mean "few."

Proportion is often mistakenly used to mean "part," or "portion." Proportion refers to a ratio.

> His spending is out of all proportion to his earnings.

If you mean "size," "dimension," or "amount," use those words.

> What are the proportions (dimensions) of your living room?
> He ate a large proportion (most) of the cake.
> A large proportion (number) of the people there smoked.

Finally:

> "Fraction" means a part of a whole — a quarter, say. If you want to emphasize the smallness of the part, then say "small fraction."

PERPETRATE/PERPETUATE

To *perpetrate* means "to commit," or "carry out," and is never followed by "on." Its most common use is in the stock phrase, "perpetrate a crime." (Hence "perpetrator.")

Do not confuse it with *perpetuate*, which means "continue" or "prolong."

> Sociologists believe there are several reasons why the poverty cycle tends to perpetuate itself.

PERSONAL/PERSONNEL

The accent is on the first syllable of *per*-son-al, and the last syllable of per-son-*nel*.

Personal means "of or relating to one's self."

Personnel is a collective noun for employees and is usually used as a plural, though it can be thought of in the singular as well. "Staff" is equally common.

> The company had too few personnel for
> the job.
> Our staff comes and goes.

(See *Collective Nouns*.)

PERSONAL/PERSONALIZED

When you are taken to your table by the owner of a restaurant, you are being given *personal* service by the owner, since he is there in person. This is not, however, *personalized* service. Personalized shirts or stationery, yes — but service cannot be initialed. *Personalized* is used to convey the sense of special, even fawning, attention — leaving *personal* sounding downright second-rate, which is untrue.

(See *Euphemisms.*)

PERSONS/PEOPLE

Some people insist that *people* is the plural of "person" and therefore the use of *persons* is incorrect. They're partly right. *People* is the plural, certainly, but if you want to emphasize the individuals — if you want to see the people as individuals — then it's quite all right to say *persons.*

> They are two of the nicest persons I've ever met.

But not:

> Fifteen million persons live in New York City.

PLUS/AND

Reserve *plus* for arithmetic and avoid using it as a synonym for "and" or "or":

> I'd like to go to Prague, plus (and) stay at Sir Toby's hostel.

> I don't want to go to Prague, plus (or) climb the Eiffel Tower.

PRACTICABLE/PRACTICAL

There is a subtle distinction between these words. *Practicable* means "capable of being performed" — feasible. *Practical* means "in accordance with reality, or current conditions."

> Thus, while it is *practicable* to tow icebergs to Africa, it is apparently not *practical* because the costs are too high.

> People can be called *practical* (or impractical) but never *practicable* (or impracticable).

PRESCRIBE/PROSCRIBE

Prescribe means recommend, *proscribe* means forbid.

> His doctor prescribed exercise and proscribed smoking.

PRINCIPAL/PRINCIPLE
Principal means first, most important.

> Lack of a steady defence was the principal
> cause of the team's loss.

Principle means a basic truth or law by which the conduct of any organized system is governed.

> Freedom within the law is a principle of
> democracy.

Remember the importance given to your pal, the *principal*, at school.

PROSECUTE/PERSECUTE
To *prosecute* means to take action under the law — "trespassers will be prosecuted."

To *persecute* means to harass (even to the point of physical attack) by denying the right of an individual, race, or organization to exist as it pleases.

PROVED/PROVEN
As the past participle of "prove," either word is correct.

They haven't *proven* anything.
They weren't *proved* guilty.

QUIET/QUITE

Yikes! It's not identical sounds that create confusion here, but the different order of the same five letters. Note that *quite* contains the word "quit." It's a good way to remember the difference.

REGARDLESS/IRREGARDLESS

Sorry, but there's no such word as *irregardless*, likely a confusion with "irrespective," which is legitimate.

REQUISITE/PREREQUISITE

Requisite means necessary — "Does he have the requisite number of courses for graduation?"

Prerequisite means "a prior condition," or "necessary before" — Basket Weaving 101 is a *prerequisite* for (not *before*) "Basket Weaving 201."

RESIDENTS/RESIDENCE

A city is inhabited by its *residents*, who call their apartment or house their *residence*, so no wonder these two words are confusing.

Residents reside in their residences. Repeat that to a stranger on the street!

ROMAN NUMERALS

When used to indicate a copyright date, as they frequently are with films, roman numerals are capitalized. When used to number the preliminary pages of a book, they are not capitalized (i, ii, iii, etc.).

1 to 20:

I	XXI — 21
II	XXX — 30
III	XL — 40
IV	L — 50
V	LX — 60
VI	LXX — 70
VII	LXXX — 80
VIII	XC — 90
IX	C — 100
X	CC — 200
XI	CCC — 300
XII	CD — 400
XIII	D — 500
XIV	DC — 600
XV	DCC — 700
XVI	DCCC — 800
XVII	CM — 900
XVIII	M — 1000

| XIX | MM — 2000 |
| XX | MMM — 3000 |

2005? MMV

SITE/CITE/SIGHT

A *site* is a particular location. To *cite* is to give a particular example.

Sight has to do with seeing.

> City Hall is built on the site of an eighteenth-century fort.

> When comparing the lower salaries of today with those of the 1990s, she cited the "tulip bulb" mania as the end of the second millennium approached.

> In Copenhagen they saw a lot of beautiful sights.

SOUND ALIKES (HOMONYMS)

These are words that have the same pronunciation, and sometimes the same spelling, but which have different meanings. A number of frequently confused sound-alike words (homonyms) are sorted out in this book under their own headings. Other sound-alike words, which are often sources of spelling errors, follow.

ad (advertisement), add
aisle, isle (island)
altar, alter (verb — "change")
ante (before), anti (against)
auger (the tool), augur (bode)
awful, offal (waste parts of a butchered animal)
bail, bale (of hay)
bait, bate (with bated breath)
better, bettor (he who bets)
borough, burrow (rabbit's hole)
breach (of promise), breech (part of a rifle)

cannon (weapon), canon (religious)
canvas (material), canvass (solicit)
cereal (grain), serial (repeated)
cue, queue (line of people)
cymbal (musical instrument), symbol

dam, damn (damn it!)
dual (pair, side by side), duel (pistols at 20 paces)

flu (influenza), flue (of a chimney)
flow, floe (ice floe)

gorilla (animal), guerrilla (soldier)

heal (get better), heel (of your foot)
hoard (like a miser), horde (of barbarians)

jam, jamb (door jamb)

magnate (shipping magnate), magnet
meat, meet, mete (mete out justice)
medal, meddle (interfere)
metal, mettle (courage)
miner (in the ground), minor (small)
moose, mousse (chocolate mousse)
mucous (that which produces mucus), mucus
   (substance produced by the mucous membrane)
muscle, mussel (shellfish)

naval, navel (belly button)

oar (of a boat), ore (iron ore)

pain, pane (of glass)
pair (two), pare (paring knife), pear (fruit)
patience, patients (doctors' patients)
peak (summit), peek (a sly look)
peal (of bells), peel (of an orange)
populace (population), populous (populated)
pore (pore over a book), pour
pray (for rain), prey (victim)

rack (spice rack), wrack (wracked with pain)

reek (smell strongly), wreak (inflict punishment)
review, revue (a musical show)
rote (by heart), wrote

shear (a lamb), sheer (steep)
sleight (of hand), slight (small)
sloe (sloe gin), slow
sole (fish), soul
straight, strait (straitjacket)
sum (total), some

vain (too proud), vane (weather vane), vein (of ore)

SPAYED/SPADE

To *spay* an animal is to remove its ovaries. When that is done, the animal is "spayed."

A common error is to say "spade" and "spaded." A spade is a shovel.

STALACTITE/STALAGMITE

You may have seen these only in photographs of caves, but they are calcite formations caused by the drip, drip, drip of mineral-rich water over eons of time.

Stalactites are the icicle-like formations that project from the roof of the cave and *stalagmites* are the broad, cylindrical deposits on its floor.

STATIONARY/STATIONERY

The first means stopped, not moving — "The economy is *stationary*."

The second refers to letters and writing materials — "She has some beautiful personalized *stationery*."

SUBTLE/SUBTLY/SUBTLETY

Understandably, it's difficult to keep the spellings of these words straight.

Subtle is an adjective:

> Among blended Scotches there are very subtle differences.

Subtly is an adverb:

> Subtly hinting that it was time for them to go, the host pretended to fall asleep.

Subtlety is a noun:

> Mussolini was not known for his subtlety.

THANK YOU
This is always written as two words, unhyphenated. When used to close a letter, the "t" is capitalized and the "you" is followed by a comma.

THEY'RE/THERE/THEIR
They're is easy — it's the contraction of "they are." (See *Apostrophe*.)

There is the opposite of "here."

Their is the possessive form of "they" as in "That's their house." If you have trouble with this one, notice that the first three letters spell "the."

Keep this sentence in mind: "They're now buying their groceries there."

TOWARD/TOWARDS
Either spelling is acceptable. So too for "upward/upwards" and "downward/downwards."

TRANSPIRE
Transpire does not mean "happen," the sense in which it is generally used. It means "to become known."

It transpired that this was not his first
conviction.

If you're tempted to say, "What transpired while I
was gone?" resist it.

TRY TO/TRY AND

While some people grit their teeth at "try and" and
insist that the correct form is "try to," there is a
subtle yet useful difference between them. If you are
having trouble getting the lid off a jar of pickles, you
would probably say, "Try to open this for me, will
you?"; whereas, exasperated that the junk in the
backyard hasn't yet been carted away, you would
say, "Try and get it done, will you?" The point is that
try and suits a promise or a nudging request, while
try to has the sense of practicability about it.

TWO/TO/TOO

Two is the number (2).

To is a preposition, like "in," "on," etc. — "I'm going
to the store."

Too has two meanings: it means "also" — "Are you
coming to the store, *too*?" — and it means
"excessive," — "I can't sleep because it's *too* hot."

Too is always used in a negative sense — "too tired to work," "too lazy to play," "too miserable for words."

Do not confuse this use of *too* with the word "very," which means a high degree, but not necessarily an unwelcome one.

> It's a very warm day, but it's never too warm for a barbeque.

UNIQUE

Because uniqueness is rare, we prize it, and therefore like to use phrases such as "rather unique," "not as unique," and "more unique." However, the word means "one of a kind," and thus there are no degrees of uniqueness. A thing is unique or it isn't, and that's that.

UNTHAW/DETHAW

These errors are both inventive confusions, inspired by the memory that "un-" and "de-" are negative prefixes, as in "unhinge" and "deconstruct."

Sometimes the mind will compound the confusion (and the error) by coming up with "unfreeze."

This is a lot of fun, and a good try, but *thaw* is the opposite of "freeze," and the correct word.

USE TO/USED TO

Did you *use to* go bowling on Friday night, or did you *used to* go?

Since you gave up bowling, are you *use to* watching TV on Friday night, or are you *used to* watching TV on Friday night?

Used to is the correct form in each of the examples above, but the meaning is obviously different. The first means "habitually in the past" and the second means "accustomed to."

> He used to be very athletic and now he can't get used to watching the world at play.

Note the different structure in these two examples:

> Lee used to play badminton.
> (Subject + used to + infinitive verb)

> Lee is used to playing badminton on Monday nights.
> (Subject + verb "to be" + used to +
> -ing form of verb)

VERBAL/ORAL/AURAL

Verbal refers to any manner of communicating language. Thus, sign language is verbal communication, as is a red light.

Oral refers only to the spoken word. A person using sign language might have considerable verbal skills but little oral facility. Written and oral communications are both verbal.

Aural (pronounced "oral") refers to listening and hearing, as in "aural comprehension."

WEATHER/WHETHER

"The *weather* has been so unpredictable recently that I can never decide *whether* to wear long pants or short pants."
(See *If/Whether*.)

WELSH/WELCH

Either spelling is acceptable, although the former is the original. To *welsh* means to fail to pay a debt or to renege on a deal. It does not mean "to squeal on somebody," a sense with which it is sometimes confused. The origin is unknown.

A native of Wales is Welsh.

WHO'S/WHOSE

Who's is a contraction of "who is" and *whose* is a relative pronoun indicating possession.

> Who's at the door?
> Whose footsteps do I hear at the door?

WORRIED/WORRISOME

> Stanley is worried about his cats, as usual.
> Although he loves them, Stanley finds his cats worrisome.

Worrisome, meaning "causing anxiety," is used to describe a situation or circumstance and cannot be used as a verb.

WOULD OF/COULD OF

This confusion is an understandable but unacceptable error resulting from mistaking "'ve" for "of." All of the following are contractions with the verb "have":

> should've
> could've
> would've

might've
had've

If you've ever made the mistake, you should've known better.

YOU'RE/YOUR

You're is no more interchangeable with *your* than "they're" is with "their" or "she's" is with "her."

You're is a contraction of "you are" and *your* is the possessive form of "you."

> "At this company, we like you to think that you're your own boss," his boss told him on the first day.